Better Homes and Gardens®

AFGHAN-STITCH CROCHET

© Copyright 1989 by Meredith Corporation, Des Moines, Iowa.
All Rights Reserved. Printed in the United States of America.
First Edition. Second Printing, 1991.
Library of Congress Catalog Card Number: 89-60205
ISBN: 0-696-01785-7 (hard cover)
ISBN: 0-696-01786-5 (trade paperback)

BETTER HOMES AND GARDENS® BOOKS

Editor: Gerald M. Knox
Art Director: Ernest Shelton
Managing Editor: David A. Kirchner
Editorial Project Managers: Liz Anderson,
    James D. Blume, Marsha Jahns,
    Jennifer Speer Ramundt, Angela K. Renkoski

Crafts Editor: Sara Jane Treinen
Senior Crafts Editors: Beverly Rivers,
    Patricia M. Wilens
Associate Crafts Editor: Nancy Reames

Associate Art Directors: Neoma Thomas,
    Linda Ford Vermie, Randall Yontz
Assistant Art Directors: Lynda Haupert,
    Harijs Priekulis, Tom Wegner
Graphic Designers: Mary Schlueter Bendgen,
    Mike Burns, Brenda Lesch
Art Production: Director, John Berg;
    Associate, Joe Heuer;
    Office Manager, Michaela Lester

President, Book Group: Jeramy Lanigan
Vice President, Retail Marketing: Jamie L. Martin
Vice President, Administrative Services: Rick Rundall

BETTER HOMES AND GARDENS® MAGAZINE
President, Magazine Group: James A. Autry
Editorial Director: Doris Eby
Editorial Services Director: Duane L. Gregg

MEREDITH CORPORATION OFFICERS
Chairman of the Executive Committee: E. T. Meredith III
Chairman of the Board: Robert A. Burnett
President: Jack D. Rehm

AFGHAN-STITCH CROCHET
Editor: Sara Jane Treinen
Editorial Project Manager: Angela K. Renkoski
Graphic Designer: Linda Ford Vermie
Contributing Graphic Designer: Patricia Konecny
Electronic Text Processor: Paula Forest

Cover project: See page 67.

CONTENTS

If you're a beginner at afghan-stitch crochet, start your adventure in this crochet technique by creating a spectacular nine-paneled afghan. You'll begin with the basic afghan-stitch panel, embroider a lovely cross-stitch motif on top of its surface, and then proceed to work eight more panels using eight different pattern stitches.

For stitchers who love to make crocheted items for gifts, here's a chapter of 17 great projects, including lingerie and small totes for your traveling friends, sachet pillows, a lovely runner for a plain or fancy table, useful country place mats, smart and comfy scarf sets, and two spectacular sweaters. The projects use some of the stitches you've already learned (if you've made the afghan in Chapter 1), plus other stitches that make crocheting fun and intriguing.

Creating handmade items for youngsters is a crafter's greatest delight. In this chapter is a collection of kids' sweaters, caps and mittens, an afghan, and a snowsuit. Most of the projects work up quickly, can fit lots of small sizes, and are guaranteed to please.

For novices and experts, this chapter offers eight afghans and throws to stitch that will catch the onlooker off-guard. Even the easy-to-stitch ones look complicated. Here are fisherman-style afghans that mimic the fantastic knitted ones, colorful patchwork quilt designs that use the basic afghan stitch, and more afghans that use the traditional method of working cross-stitch motifs on the surface of the stitching.

A SAMPLER AFGHAN

A STITCH IN TIME MAKES NINE

Begin your adventure into afghan-stitch crochet by making the 48x65-inch afghan at *left.* You'll learn the basic afghan stitch and eight other pattern stitches. Each panel of the afghan is worked in a different pattern stitch. After all the panels are made, crochet them together, and add the fringe. Once you've mastered all these pattern stitches, you'll be ready to proceed with the other projects in this book.

Included in this chapter are tips and diagrams to provide you with more information about this unique and intriguing method of crocheting. There also are drawings to show you how to work increases and decreases.

We'll tell you about hooks and all the sizes they come in. Throughout the book you'll discover more interesting patterns and stitch textures and learn how to work projects with more than one color.

MATERIALS

Aarlan Royal (50-gram ball) in the following amounts and colors: 12 balls of ecru (No. 4324), 5 balls *each* of light heather blue (No. 4254) and medium heather blue (No. 4304)

Size H afghan-crochet hook

Abbreviations: See list, *opposite.*
Gauge: Each side strip is 5 inches wide before blocking; the center panel is 8 inches wide.

Basic Afghan-Stitch Pattern

The center panel of the afghan features the basic afghan stitch with the traditional cross-stitch embellishments. Once you master this stitch, all other stitch variations are easier to understand and work.

As you work the afghan stitch, you'll always stitch with the right side facing you. Never turn the work unless directed otherwise in the instructions. All stitch patterns follow the same basic technique. There are two steps to each row. In this book, the first step is always referred to as the "first half" of the row, and the second step is named the "second half."

On the first half of the row, you work from right to left into the stitches of the previous row, picking up loops and keeping these loops on the hook. On the second half, you work from left to right, and remove the loops from the hook. It is this back-and-forth stitching that creates all afghan-stitch patterns.

1 CENTER PANEL: With ecru yarn and afghan hook, ch 37.
Row 1 (first half): Referring to drawing *above,* insert the hook in the top lp of the second ch from the hook, yo (wrap the yarn around the hook), draw the yarn through the chain and leave the lp on the hook—2 lps on the hook; * insert the hook in the top lp of the *next* ch, yo, draw the yarn through the chain and leave the lp on the hook; rep from the * across the row—37 lps on hook.

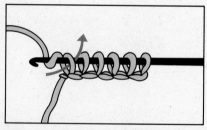

2 *Row 1 (second half):* Working from left to right, yo, draw the yarn through the *first* lp on the hook (see drawing *above*).

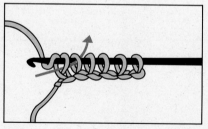

3 * Yo, draw the yarn through 2 lps on the hook; rep from the * across the row until 1 lp rem on hook. This last lp counts as the first stitch of the next row.

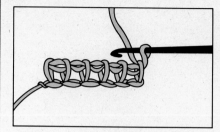

4 At the end of the first row, the work will look like the drawing *above.* Notice the upright *bars* or *lps.* These bars form the foundation for working pattern stitches in subsequent rows.

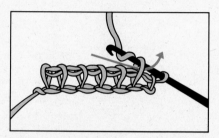

5 *Row 2 (first half):* Referring to drawing *above,* sk the first upright bar; * insert the hook behind the *front* lp of the next upright bar, yo, draw the yarn through the bar and leave the lp on the hook; rep from the * across the row—37 lps on the hook.
Note: The instructions between the *s in Row 2 will be abbreviated and read "draw up lp in next bar" in the pattern stitches that follow.
Row 2 (second half): Rep the second half of Row 1.
Rep Row 2 (first and second halves) to make 209 rows.

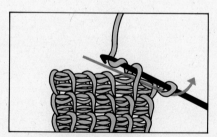

6 *Last row* (bind-off row): Sk the first upright bar, * **insert the hook in front of the next bar, yo, draw the yarn through the bar and through the lp on the hook—sl st made and 1 lp on hook;** rep from the * across the row; fasten off.

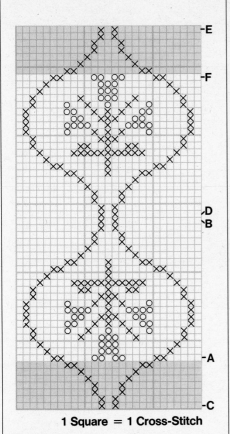

1 Square = 1 Cross-Stitch

COLOR KEY
⊠ Light Blue   ⊙ Medium Blue

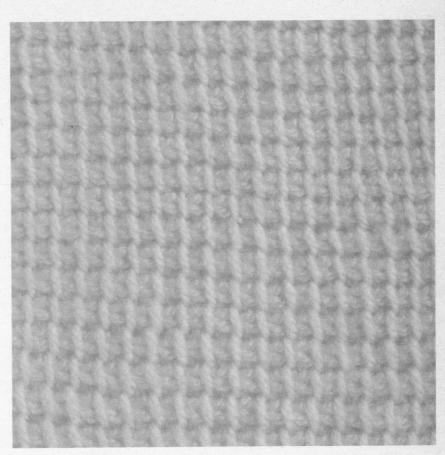

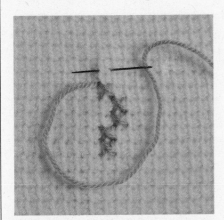

FOR THE CROSS-STITCHING: Referring to the chart *above,* use one strand of yarn to work the cross-stitches on the center 25 stitches. Beginning at the bottom of the strip, work from A–B once; work from C–B three times; work from D–E three times; then work from D–F once. The photo *above* shows how the cross-stitches are worked on top of the basic af-ghan-stitch panel.

Abbreviations

beg	begin(ning)
bet	between
ch(s)	chain(s)
cl(s)	cluster(s)
cont	continue
dc	double crochet
dec	decrease
dpn	double-point needle
fp	front post
fps	foundation post st
hdc	half double crochet
inc	increase
k	knit
lp(s)	loop(s)
ltr	long treble crochet
MC	main color
p	purl

pat	pattern
pc	popcorn
post trc	post treble crochet
rem	remain
rep	repeat
rnd(s)	round(s)
sc	single crochet
sk	skip
sl st	slip stitch

Lattice Pattern

With ecru, ch 23.

Row 1 (first half): Keeping all lps on hook, insert hook in top lp of second ch from hook, yo, draw up lp; * insert hook in top lp of next ch, yo, draw up lp; rep from * across row—23 lps on hook.

Row 1 (second half): Yo, draw yarn through first lp on hook; * yo, draw yarn through 2 lps on hook; rep from * across row until 1 lp rem on hook.

Row 2 (first half): Keeping all lps on hook, sk first bar, * insert hook in front of next bar and draw up lp; rep from * across—23 lps on hook.

Row 2 (second half): Rep second half of Row 1.

Row 3: Rep first and second halves of Row 2.

Row 4 (first half): Keeping all lps on hook, sk first bar, draw up lp in each of next 2 bars; * sk next bar, draw up lp in next bar, draw up lp in skipped bar to right; rep from * across; ending draw up lp in last 2 bars.

Row 4 (second half): Rep second half of Row 1.

Rep Row 4 (first and second halves) for pat until a total of 207 rows are worked.

Rows 208 and 209: Rep Row 2 (first and second halves).

Last row (bind-off row): Sk the first upright bar; referring to the drawing above Step 6 on page 6, * **insert the hook in front of the next bar, yo, draw the yarn through the bar and through the lp on the hook—sl st made and 1 lp on hook;** rep from the * across the row; fasten off.

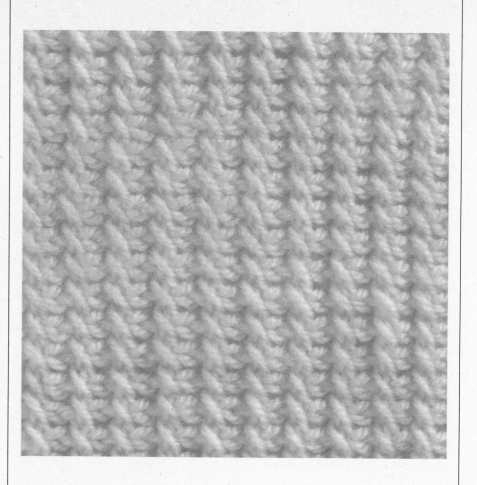

An Introduction To Afghan-Stitch Crochet

Often referred to as Tunisian crochet or tricot crochet, the basic afghan stitch (as used in the center panel of this afghan) has been a part of the crochet repertoire for centuries. Its popularity in early times, which continues today, is due to the beautiful cross-stitch embellishments that easily can be worked over the tiny squares of the even-weave pattern.

Many patterns of afghan crochet also resemble those of knitting—that's why it's often called tricot (French word for knitting) crochet. Only upon close examination can the viewer determine the fabric is knitted on a crochet hook. There are patterns for purl stitches, cable stitches, lacy stitches, and raised stitches.

Afghan crochet has a wonderful assortment of interesting textures that produces spectacular results, not only for exquisite afghans but also for sweaters, caps, scarves, mittens, pillows, sachets, and more.

If this crochet technique is new to you, practice making swatches of patterns before you begin your project. You'll want to develop a consistent tension on the yarn to keep your work straight and even—not too tight, not too loose. Notice how the stitches look different on the wrong side (back side) of the work. As you develop your skill, your swatch will have the same width measurement across its bottom, middle, and top.

Basket-Weave Pattern

With light blue, ch 23.

Row 1 (first half): Keeping all lps on hook, insert hook in top lp of second ch from hook, yo, draw up lp; * insert hook in top lp of next ch, yo, draw up lp; rep from * across row—23 lps on hook.

Row 1 (second half): Yo, draw through first lp on hook; * yo, draw through 2 lps on hook; rep from * across row until 1 lp rem on hook.

Row 2 (first half): Keeping all lps on hook, sk first bar, * insert hook in next bar and draw up lp; rep from * across row—23 lps on hook.

Row 2 (second half): Rep second half of Row 1.

Row 3: Rep first and second halves of Row 2.

Row 4 (first half): Keeping all lps on hook, sk first bar, draw up lp in each of next 3 bars; referring to drawing *below,* * **bring yarn to**

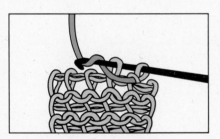

front of work and hold yarn below the row you are working in; (insert hook in next bar, yo, draw up lp) 3 times—3 p sts made; take yarn to back and draw up lp in each of next 3 bars; rep from * across; end draw up lp in last 4 bars.

Row 4 (second half): Rep second half of Row 1.

Rows 5 and 6: Rep first and second halves of Row 4.

Row 7 (first half): Sk first bar, * bring yarn to front and work p sts in each of next 3 bars; take yarn to back and draw up lp in each of next 3 bars; rep from * across row; end row with 3 p sts, take yarn to back and draw up lp in last bar.

Row 7 (second half): Rep second half of Row 1.

Rows 8 and 9: Rep first and second halves of Row 7.

Rep rows 4–9 for 33 more times until a total of 207 rows are worked.

Rows 208 and 209: Rep Row 2 working in basic afghan stitch.

Last row (bind-off row): Sk the first upright bar; referring to the drawing above Step 6 on page 6, * **insert the hook in front of the next bar, yo, draw the yarn through the bar and through the lp on the hook—sl st made and 1 lp on hook;** rep from the * across the row; fasten off.

Mock Cable Pattern

With ecru, ch 23.

Row 1 (first half): Keeping all lps on hook, insert hook in top lp of second ch from hook, yo, draw up lp; * insert hook in top lp of next ch, yo, draw up lp; rep from * across row—23 lps on hook.

Row 1 (second half): Yo, draw through first lp on hook; * yo, draw through 2 lps on hook; rep from * across row until 1 lp rem on hook.

Row 2 (first half): Keeping all lps on hook, sk first bar, * insert hook in front of next bar and draw up lp; rep from * across—23 lps on hook.

Row 2 (second half): Rep second half of Row 1.

Row 3: Rep first and second halves of Row 2.

Row 4 (first half): Keeping all lps on hook, sk first 2 bars; * draw up lp in next bar; draw up lp in skipped bar to right; bring yarn forward and work p st in next bar; take yarn to back, sk next bar; rep from * across; draw up lp in last bar.

Row 4 (second half): Rep second half of Row 1.

Row 5 (first half): Keeping all lps on hook, sk first bar; * bring yarn forward and work p st in each of next 2 bars; take yarn back and draw up lp in next bar; rep from * across; end draw up lp in last bar.

Row 5 (second half): Rep second half of Row 1.

Rep rows 4 and 5 (first and second halves) for pattern until 207 rows are completed.

Rows 208 and 209: Rep Row 2 working in basic afghan stitch.

Last row (bind-off row): Sk the first upright bar; referring to the drawing above Step 6 on page 6, * **insert the hook in front of the next bar, yo, draw the yarn through the bar and through the lp on the hook—sl st made and 1 lp on hook;** rep from the * across the row; fasten off.

Working Increases In Afghan-Stitch Crochet

Increasing makes your crochet piece wider or fuller. In most instances, increasing is used for garment shaping—to make the sleeves wider, for example. Increases are usually made at the beginning and the end of a row, but sometimes they are worked within the row. The instructions will specify where and when they occur.

In afghan stitch, the increases are always made while working the first half of the row (the row when you pick up loops and place them on the hook). It's wise to count the number of loops on the hook at the end of an "increase" row to make certain you have the correct number of stitches.

To increase a stitch at the beginning of a row, skip the first up-

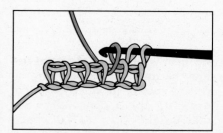

right bar, draw up a loop in the next bar; referring to the drawing *above,* draw up a loop in the space (under the chain) before the next bar—1 stitch increased. Continue across the row in the pattern stitch, drawing up lps in each bar until 2 bars remain at the end of the row.

To increase a stitch at the end of a row, draw up a loop under the chain before the next bar—1 stitch increased. Draw up 2 loops in the remaining 2 bars.

Ribbed Pattern

With medium blue, ch 23.

Row 1 (first half): Keeping all lps on hook, insert hook in top lp of second ch from hook, yo, draw up lp; * insert hook in top lp of next ch, yo, draw up lp; rep from * across row—23 lps on hook.

Row 1 (second half): Yo, draw yarn through first lp on hook; * yo, draw through 2 lps on hook; rep from * across row until 1 lp rem on hook.

Row 2 (first half): Keeping all lps on hook, sk first bar; referring to drawing on page 9, * bring **yarn to front of work and hold yarn below the row you are working in, insert hook in next bar, yo, draw up lp—p st made;** take yarn back and draw up lp in next bar; rep from * across row.

Row 2 (second half): Rep second half of Row 1.

Rep Row 2 (first and second halves) for pattern until total of 208 rows are worked.

Row 209: Rep Row 2 working in basic afghan stitch.

Last row (bind-off row): Sk the first upright bar; referring to drawing above Step 6 on page 6 * **insert the hook in the next bar, yo, draw the yarn through the bar and through the lp on the hook—sl st made and 1 lp on hook;** rep from the * across the row; fasten off.

Working Decreases In Afghan-Stitch Crochet

Decreasing makes your crochet piece narrower. Like increases, decreases are used to shape crocheted fabric—to make a mitten or cap narrower at the finger tips or crown, for example. Decreases, too, are usually made at the beginning and the end of a row, but often they are worked within the row. The instructions will specify where and when they occur.

In afghan stitch, the decreases are always made while working the first half of the row (the row when you pick up loops and place them on the hook). Count the number of loops on the hook at the end of a "decrease" row to make certain you have the correct number of stitches.

To decrease a stitch at the beginning of a row, skip the first up-

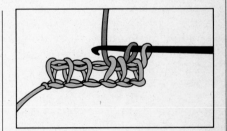

right bar; referring to the drawing *above,* insert the hook in front of the next 2 bars, and draw up 1 loop—1 stitch decreased. Continue across the row in the pattern stitch, drawing up lps in each bar until 3 bars remain at the end of the row.

To decrease a stitch at the end of a row, insert the hook in front of the next 2 bars, and draw up 1 loop—1 stitch decreased. Draw up loop in the remaining bar.

NINE-PANEL STRIP AFGHAN

Raised Horizontal Pattern

With medium blue, ch 23.

Row 1 (first half): Keeping all lps on hook, insert hook in top lp of second ch from hook, yo, draw up lp; * insert hook in top lp of next ch, yo, draw up lp; rep from * across row—23 lps on hook.

Row 1 (second half): Yo, draw through first lp on hook; * yo, draw through 2 lps on hook; rep from * across row until 1 lp rem on hook.

Row 2 (first half): Keeping all lps on hook, sk first bar, *** bring yarn to front of work and hold yarn below the row you are working in, insert hook in next bar, yo, draw up lp—p st made;** rep from * across—23 lps on hook.

Row 2 (second half): Rep second half of Row 1.

Row 3 (first half): Keeping all lps on hook, sk first bar, draw up lp in next bar; * sk next bar, draw up lp in next bar, draw up lp in skipped bar; rep from * across row; end draw up lp in last bar.

Row 3 (second half): Rep second half of Row 1.

Row 4 (first half): Keeping all lps on hook, sk first bar; * draw up lp in next bar; rep from * across row.

Row 4 (second half): Rep second half of Row 1.

Rep rows 2–4 for pattern until total of 208 rows are worked.

Row 209: Rep Row 4.

Last row (bind-off row): Sk the first upright bar, *** insert the hook in the next bar, yo, draw the yarn through the bar and through the lp on the hook—sl st made and 1 lp on hook;** rep from the * across the row; fasten off.

Afghan-Stitch Hooks

Afghan-stitch crochet uses hooks that are longer than regular crochet hooks. These hooks look like knitting needles except they have hooks at the pointed ends. There are no finger indent places on afghan hooks for resting your fingers. Hooks come in 9- and 14-inch lengths, and there are flexible ones that can hold even more stitches. Longer hooks are necessary in order to hold all the stitches that are picked up on the first half of the row.

Like crochet hooks, afghan hooks are made of aluminum or plastic. Their sizes are designated with numbers or letters—the lower the number, the smaller the size. The hook and shank portions of the hooks become larger as the sizes of the hooks increase.

Because hooks have both letter and number sizes—some patterns call for a Size G hook, and other patterns call for a Size 6—the equivalents of both designators are as follows:

Hook Equivalents	
Letter Size	Numeric Size
E	4
F	5
G	6
H	8
I	9
J	10
K	10.5

Fabric Pattern

With ecru, ch 23.

Row 1 (first half): Keeping all lps on hook, insert hook in top lp of second ch from hook, yo, draw up lp; * insert hook in top lp of next ch, yo, draw up lp; rep from * across row—23 lps on hook.

Row 1 (second half): Yo, draw through first lp on hook; * yo, draw through 2 lps on hook; rep from * across row until 1 lp rem on hook.

Row 2 (first half): Keeping all lps on hook, sk first bar, * insert hook in next bar and draw up lp; rep from * across—23 lps on hook.

Row 2 (second half): Rep second half of Row 1.

Row 3: Rep first and second halves of Row 2.

Row 4 (first half): Keeping all lps on hook, sk first bar; * sk next bar, draw up lp in next bar, draw up lp in skipped bar; rep from * across.

Row 4 (second half): Rep second half of Row 1.

Row 5 (first half): Keeping all lps on hook, sk first bar; draw up lp in next bar; * sk next bar, draw up lp in next bar, draw up lp in skipped bar; rep from * across; end draw up lp in last bar.

Row 5 (second half): Rep second half of Row 1.

Rep rows 4 and 5 for pattern until 207 rows are worked.

Rows 208 and 209: Rep Row 2, working in basic afghan stitch.

Last row (bind-off row): Sk the first upright bar, * **insert the hook in next upright bar, yo, draw the yarn through the bar and through the lp on the hook—sl st made and 1 lp on hook;** rep from the * across the row; fasten off.

Stitching Multicolored Designs With Afghan Stitch

You can create wonderful designs by stitching with two or more colors. (See the afghans on pages 62 and 63 and the child's sweater on page 40.) Depending on your pattern, color can change in the middle *or* at the beginning of a row.

When changing color in the middle of a row, work across the *first half* of the row using the first color and picking up the required number of stitches. Drop the yarn in use to the back of the work. With the second color, pick up the required number of stitches. If any two colors are used alternately and they have fewer than four stitches between them, you can carry the yarn across the back of the work. If more than three or four stitches are between each color, use bobbins and carry separate balls of yarn colors.

On the *second half* of the row, take the loops off the hook until one loop before the next color remains on the hook; drop the yarn to the back of the work. Then, with the second color, take the two different-colored loops from the hook and remove the loops in that color until 1 loop of that color remains before the next color change. Continue across the row in this manner until one loop remains on the hook.

When changing yarn colors at the beginning of the row, work the *second half* of the row until two loops remain on the hook. Drop the color in use to the back of the work, and complete the row with the second color.

Chevron Pattern

With light blue, ch 23.

Row 1 (first half): Keeping all lps on hook, insert hook in top lp of second ch from hook, yo, draw up lp; * insert hook in top lp of next ch, yo, draw up lp; rep from * across row—23 lps on hook.

Row 1 (second half): Yo, draw through first lp on hook; * yo, draw through 2 lps on hook; rep from * across row until 1 lp rem on hook.

Row 2 (first half): Keeping all lps on hook, sk first bar, * insert hook in next bar and draw up lp; rep from * across—23 lps on hook.

Row 2 (second half): Rep second half of Row 1.

Row 3: Rep first and second halves of Row 2.

Row 4 (first half): Keeping all lps on hook, sk first bar; * draw up lp in each of next 3 bars; **bring yarn to front of work and hold yarn below the row you are working in; (insert hook in next bar, yo, draw up lp) 3 times—3 p sts made;** take yarn to back and rep from * across; end take yarn to back and draw up lp last 4 bars.

Row 4 (second half and all subsequent second halves of rows): Rep second half of Row 1.

Row 5 (first half): Keeping all lps on hook, sk first bar; **bring yarn to front of work and hold yarn below the row you are working in, insert hook in next bar, yo, draw up lp—p st made;** * take yarn to back and draw up lp in each of next 3 bars; bring yarn to front and work p st in each of next 3 bars; rep from * across row; end draw up lp in last 3 bars.

Row 6 (first half): Keeping all lps on hook, sk first bar; bring yarn to front and work p st in each of next 2 bars; * take yarn to back and draw up lp in each of next 3 bars; bring yarn to front and work p st in each of next 3 bars; rep from * across; end take yarn to back and draw up lps in each of last 2 bars.

Row 7 (first half): Keeping all lps on hook, sk first bar; * bring yarn to front and work p st in each of next 3 bars; take yarn to back and draw up lp in each of next 3 bars; rep from * across; end take yarn to back and draw up lp in last bar.

Row 8 (first half): Keeping all lps on hook, sk first bar; draw up lp in next bar; * bring yarn to front and work p st in each of next 3 bars; take yarn to back and draw up lp in each of next 3 bars; rep from * across to last 3 bars; work p sts in each of last 3 bars.

Row 9 (first half): Keeping all lps on hook, sk first bar; draw up lp in each of next 2 bars; * bring yarn to front and work p st in each of next 3 bars; take yarn to back and draw up lp in each of next 3 bars; rep from * across; end draw up 2 p sts in last 2 bars.

Rep rows 4–9 (33 more times) for pattern until 207 rows are completed.

Rows 208 and 209: Rep Row 2 working in basic afghan stitch.

Last row (bind-off row): Sk the first upright bar, * **insert the hook in next upright bar, yo, draw the yarn through the bar and through the lp on the hook—sl st made and 1 lp on hook;** rep from the * across the row; fasten off.

Honeycomb Pattern

With ecru, ch 23.

Row 1 (first half): Keeping all lps on hook, insert hook in top lp of second ch from hook, yo, draw up lp; * insert hook in top lp of next ch, yo, draw up lp; rep from * across row—23 lps on hook.

Row 1 (second half): Yo, draw through first lp on hook; * yo, draw through 2 lps on hook; rep from * across row until 1 lp rem on hook.

Row 2 (first half): Keeping all lps on hook, sk first bar, * insert hook in next bar and draw up lp; rep from * across—23 lps on hook.

Row 2 (second half): Rep second half of Row 1.

Row 3: Rep first and second halves of Row 2.

Row 4 (first half): Keeping all lps on hook, sk first bar, draw up lp in next bar; * **bring yarn to front of work and hold yarn below the row you are working in, insert hook in next bar, yo, draw up lp in next bar—p st made;** take yarn to back and draw up lp in next bar; rep from * across; end draw up lp in last 2 bars.

Row 4 (second half): Rep second half of Row 1.

Row 5 (first half): Keeping all lps on hook, sk first bar; * bring yarn to front and work p st in next bar; take yarn to back and draw up lp in next bar; rep from * across; end draw up lp in last bar.

Row 5 (second half): Rep second half of Row 1.

Rep rows 4 and 5 for pattern until total of 207 rows are worked.

Rows 208 and 209: Rep Row 2, working in basic afghan stitch.

Last row (bind-off row): Sk the first upright bar, * **insert the hook in the next bar, yo, draw the yarn through the bar and through the lp on the hook—sl st made and 1 lp on hook;** rep from the * across the row; fasten off.

FINISHING: Afghan-stitch panels have a tendency to roll, so it is best to block them before putting them together. To block these panels, lay them out separately on long strips of brown or butcher paper. Lightly draw the finished blocked size of each strip on the paper. With sewing thread, attach the strips to the paper with long running stitches, stretching the panels when necessary to measure the finished size. Lay damp towels over the strips, and allow the towels to dry completely. When dry, remove the towels and basting threads, and whipstitch the panels together using one of the matching yarn colors of one of the panels.

In our afghan, the color of the fringe along the top and bottom edges of the afghan matches the color of each panel. Cut 13-inch lengths of the three yarn colors. Fold each length in half, and using a crochet hook, knot the folded lengths individually in each chain (at the bottom edge), and slip-stitch (at the top edge) across the afghan.

EXCEPTIONAL GIFTS

MAKING THE MOST OF THESE TECHNIQUES

Look what you can do with afghan-stitch crochet! Once you've mastered the basic technique, you can create any number of exciting designs for personal and home accessories. In this chapter, 14 patterns make 20 projects you can add to your afghan-stitch repertoire.

Anyone who travels is sure to treasure these crocheted totes. Crafted of soft, lustrous—yet practical—Patons Pearl Twist, these elegant bags are designed to safeguard jewelry and other trip essentials. The five bags range from 3x5½ inches to 9x11 inches. The small bags are worked in ribbing, *below right,* and a simple crossover stitch, *below left.* The larger bags feature a mesh pattern, *near right,* bobble stitch, *opposite, top,* and shell design, *opposite, far right.*

Crocheted cording, tassels, and simple edgings at the top of each bag can be worked in any accent color.

Instructions for the projects in this section begin on page 26.

EXCEPTIONAL GIFTS

Reminiscent of assisi embroidery, in which the design is left plain and the background is stitched, this floral pillow, *opposite,* features four crocheted stockinette-stitch squares embellished with duplicate stitches.

Bobble-stitch borders and rows of single crochet complete the pillow top.

The next time you need a hostess gift or any small token of your esteem and affection, think of these sachets, *above.* All three are quick and easy to stitch.

The edgings—one with hearts (lavender) and two with scallops—are interchangeable.

Fill the sachets with sweet-smelling dried flowers and herbs, then decorate them with ribbons or purchased floral appliqués.

EXCEPTIONAL GIFTS

Handcrafted place mats and coasters, or a beautifully crocheted runner, can turn even the plainest table into an inviting spot.

The colonial star mat and coaster, *above,* feature a band of traditional afghan-stitch crochet that is enhanced with cross-stitched stars. After working the band, add rows of shell stitches along the sides. The finished mat measures 13x19 inches. The coaster is 4 inches square.

The lacy table runner, *opposite,* is stitched in a simple honeycomb pattern that even a novice crocheter can master with ease. This runner measures 16x32 inches (excluding the fringe). To alter the length of the runner for your own table, simply add or subtract rows of stitches.

ooks can be deceiving. These caps, scarves, and mittens, for example, might *look* like traditional fair isle and fisherman knitting, but they're actually crocheted. When you read through the directions, you'll even find that you'll be crocheting "knit" and "purl" stitches.

Crafted of sport yarn, the hats and mittens in both designs are sized for children and adults. Youngsters' scarves will measure 7x36 inches, including the fringe. Mom's heart-bedecked scarf is 8x48 inches; Dad's cable-trimmed Aran scarf is 8x55 inches.

Get set for summer—and an occasional cool day on the golf course, in the garden, or wherever you happen to be—with an afghan-crocheted sweater embellished with bright cross-stitches.

Crochet either of these sweaters using the same instructions; only the necklines are different. The crewneck pullover *above* sports embroidered flowers, which make up just a part of the design on the sweater *opposite.*

A classic boat neck squares off the top of this sweater, making the front a perfect spot for a sampling of letters and numbers, a simple border design, and a spray of blossoms.

Stitch this sweater and its companion using pink or blue worsted-weight yarn. (Or choose another favorite color.) For the embroidery, use yarns in colors similar to those in the photos and ones that show up well against the background.

Directions are included for small, medium, and large sizes.

Lingerie Bags

Shown on pages 16–17.

Bag with bobble stitch measures 7 inches wide and 9 inches tall. Bag with shell stitch measures 8 inches wide and 10 inches tall. Mesh bag measures 9 inches wide and 11 inches tall.

MATERIALS
Patons Pearl Twist (50-gram ball): 5 balls of off-white (No. 6103) to make all 3 bags; 1 ball *each* of rose (No. 6118) and light teal (No. 6101) for trim
Sizes H and J afghan crochet hooks
Sizes C, F, and G crochet hooks
Polyester fiberfill

Abbreviations: See page 7.

INSTRUCTIONS
For the bag with bobble stitch
With H afghan hook and off-white pearl twist, ch 80.

Row 1 (first half): Keeping all lps on hook, insert hook in top lp of second ch from hook, yo, draw up lp; * insert hook in top lp of next ch, yo, draw up lp; rep from * across row—80 lps on hook.

Row 1 (second half): Yo, draw through first lp on hook; * yo, draw through 2 lps on hook; rep from * across row until 1 lp rem on hook.

Row 2 (first half): Keeping all lps on hook, sk first bar, draw up lp in each of next 3 bars; * yo, sk next bar, draw up lp in each of next 3 bars; rep from * across; end draw up lp in each of last 3 bars.

Row 2 (second half): Yo, draw yarn through 2 lps on hook; * ch 3, (yo, draw yarn through 2 lps on hook) 4 times; rep from *; end (yo, draw yarn through 2 lps) 6 times.

Row 3 (first half): Sk first bar, draw up lp in each of next 3 bars, draw up lp in slanted bar, draw up lp in next bar; * holding ch-3 at *front* of work, draw up lp in each of next 2 bars, draw up lp in slanted bar, draw up lp in next bar; rep from * across; end draw up lp in each of last 2 bars.

Row 3 (second half): Rep second half of Row 1.

Row 4 (first half): Sk first bar, draw up lp in next bar; * yo, sk bar, draw up lp in each of next 3 bars; rep from * across; end draw up lp in last 5 bars.

Row 4 (second half): (Yo, draw yarn through 2 lps) 3 times; * ch 3, (yo, draw yarn through 2 lps) 4 times; rep from * to end.

Row 5 (first half): Sk first bar, draw up lp in next bar, draw up lp in slanted bar, draw up lp in next bar; * holding ch-3 at *front* of work, draw up lp in each of next 2 bars, draw up lp in slanted bar, draw up lp in next bar; rep from * across; end draw up lp in each of last 4 bars.

Row 5 (second half): Rep second half of Row 1.

Rep rows 2–5 for pat until piece measures 7 inches; end with second half of Row 5.

Next row (first half–beading pat): Ch 1, sk first bar; * draw up lp in next bar, ch 1; rep from * across; end draw up lp in last st.

Next row (second half): Rep second half of Row 1.

Rep rows 2–5 until entire piece is 9 inches; end with second half of any row.

Bind off row: Sk first bar, * **draw up lp in next bar and draw yarn through lp on hook—sl st made and 1 lp on hook;** rep from * across; fasten off.

With wrong side facing, whipstitch side and bottom seams.

EDGING: *Rnd 1:* Working with F hook, join rose twist at side seam, ch 1, sc in same st as join and in each st around; join with sl st to first sc.

Rnd 2: Ch 1, sc in same st as join; ch 3, * sk sc, in next sc work 2 dc, ch 1, and 2 dc; sk sc, dc in next sc; rep from * around; join to sc at beg of rnd; fasten off.

CORD: With rose twist and C hook, make a chain to measure 22 inches. Sl st in second ch from hook and in each ch across; fasten off. Weave cord through beading row of bag.

TASSEL (make 2): With rose twist and C hook, ch 2. Work 5 sc in second ch from hook; do not join. Mark last st and move marker at end of each rnd to mark last st. Working in back lps, work 2 sc in each sc around—10 sc.

Next 5 rnds: Sc in back lp of each st; do not join; fasten off at end of last rnd, leaving an 8-inch tail.

Thread tail with tapestry needle and run gathering thread around top of tassel. Stuff tassel with fiberfill. Pull up gathering threads to close top and secure. Sew tassel to each end of cord.

For the bag with shell stitch
With J afghan hook and off-white twist, ch 76.

Row 1: Work 4 dc in fourth ch from hook, * sk 3 ch, sc in next ch, sk 3 ch, 9 dc in next ch; rep from * until 4 chs rem; sk 3 ch, 5 dc in last ch; ch 1, turn.

Row 2: Sc in first dc; * keeping all lps on hook, draw up lp in each of next 5 sts—6 lps on hook; draw up lp in next st and draw this lp through first lp on hook; (yo, draw yarn through 2 lps on hook) 5 times—1 lp on hook; ** keeping all lps on hook, sk first bar, draw up lp in each of next 5 bars; draw up lp in next st and draw this lp through first lp on hook; (yo, draw yarn through 2 lps on hook) 5 times; rep from ** twice more. Sk first bar, (**insert hook in next bar, yo, and draw yarn through bar and lp on hook—1 st bound off**) 5 times; sc in next st; rep from * across; end bind off 5 sts, sl st in top of turning ch; ch 1, turn.

Row 3: Sk first st, sc in each st across; end sl st in last st; ch 3, turn.

Row 4: Sk first sc; **yo, draw up lp in next sc, yo, draw through 2 lps on hook; (yo, draw up lp in next st, yo, draw through 2 lps on hook) 3 times; yo, draw through 5 lps on hook—½-shell made;** ch 1 tightly to form eye of shell; * ch 3, sc in next st, ch 3, (yo, draw up lp in next st, yo, draw through 2 lps on hook) 9 times; yo, draw through 10 lps on hook—shell made; ch 1 tightly to form eye of shell; rep from * across; end (yo, draw up lp in next st, yo, draw through 2 lps on hook) 4 times, yo, draw through 5 lps on hook, ch 1 tightly to form eye; ch 3, turn.

Row 5: 4 dc in eye of first ½-shell, sc in first sc; * 9 dc in eye of next shell, sc in next sc; rep from * across; end 5 dc in eye of last shell; ch 1, turn.

Rep rows 2–5 for pat until piece measures 7½ inches; end with Row 4; ch 1, turn.

Next row (first-half beading row): Keeping all lps on hook, draw up lp in eye of first ½-shell, ch 1; * draw up lp in first ch of ch-3 lp, ch 1, (draw up lp in next ch, ch 1) 2 times, draw up lp in eye of next shell, ch 1; rep from * across; end draw up lp in eye of last ½-shell.

Next row (second half): Yo, draw through first lp on hook; * yo, draw through 2 lps on hook; rep from * across row until 1 lp rem on hook; ch 1.

Next row: Sc in each ch-1 sp across—76 sc; ch 3, turn.

Next row: 4 dc in first sc, * sk 3 sc, sc in next sc, sk 3 sc, 9 dc in next sc; rep from * across to last 4 sc. Sk 3 sc, 5 dc in last sc; ch 1, turn.

Rep rows 2–5; fasten off.
Sew side and bottom seams.

EDGING: Working with G hook, join teal twist and work 1 rnd of reverse single crochet (sc from right to left) around top of bag; join; fasten off.

CORD: With teal twist and G hook, make a chain to measure 24 inches. Sl st in second ch from hook and in each ch across; fasten off. Weave cord through beading row of bag.

FINISHING: With teal twist and C hook, make tassels following instructions for bobble bag.

For the mesh bag
With J afghan hook and off-white twist, ch 80.

Rnd 1 (first half): Keeping all lps on hook, insert hook in top lp of second ch from hook, yo, draw up lp; * insert hook in top lp of next ch, yo, draw up lp; rep from * across row—80 lps on hook.

Row 1 (second half): Yo, draw through first lp on hook; * yo, draw through 2 lps on hook; rep from * across row until 1 lp rem on hook.

Row 2 (first half): Keeping all lps on hook, sk first bar, * **bring yarn to front of work and hold yarn below the sts you are working in, insert hook under next 2 bars, yo, draw up lp—purl 2 tog made;** take yarn back and draw up lp in sp bet last st worked and next bar; rep from * across; end draw up lp in last sp, draw up lp in last bar.

Row 2 (second half): Rep second half of Row 1.

Rep Row 2 for pat until piece measures 13 inches.

Bind off row: Sk first bar, * **draw up lp in next bar and draw yarn through lp on hook—sl st made;** rep from * across; fasten off. With wrong side facing, whipstitch side and bottom seams.

EDGING: Join rose twist at side seam, and with G hook work scs evenly spaced around top of bag; join with sl st to first sc.

Rnd 2: * Ch 3, work 4 dc in same sc as sl st, sk 3 sc, sc in next sc; rep from * around; join to first ch at beg of rnd; fasten off.

CORD: With rose twist and G hook, make chain to measure 26 inches. Sl st in second ch from hook and in each ch across; fasten off. Weave cord through beading row of bag.

FINISHING: With rose twist and C hook, make tassels following instructions for bobble bag.

Jewelry Bags

Shown on page 16.

Smaller bag measures 3 inches wide and 5½ inches tall.
Larger bag measures 4½ inches wide and 7¼ inches tall.

MATERIALS
Patons Pearl Twist (50-gram ball): 1 ball *each* of off-white (No. 6103), rose (No. 6118), and light teal (No. 6101)
Size G afghan crochet hook
Sizes C and F crochet hooks
Polyester fiberfill

Abbreviations: See page 7.

INSTRUCTIONS
For the smaller bag
With afghan hook and off-white twist, ch 36.

Row 1 (first half): Keeping all lps on hook, insert hook in top lp of second ch from hook, yo, draw up lp; * insert hook in top lp of next ch, yo, draw up lp; rep from * across row—36 lps on hook.

Row 1 (second half): Yo, draw through first lp on hook; * yo, draw through 2 lps on hook; rep from * across row until 1 lp rem on hook.

Row 2 (first half): Keeping all lps on hook, sk first bar, * **bring yarn to front of work and hold yarn below the st you are working in, draw up lp in next bar— purl st made;** take yarn back and **insert hook from front to back bet the next vertical lp (bet front and back upright bars), draw up lp—knit st made;** rep from * across; end draw up lp in last bar.

Row 2 (second half): Rep second half of Row 1.

Rep Row 2 for pat for 4 inches.

Next row (first half–beading pat): Ch 1, sk first bar; * draw up lp in next bar, ch 1; rep from * across; end draw up lp in last st.

Next row (second half): Rep second half of Row 1.

Rep Row 2 for 1 inch; end with second half of Row 2.

continued

Binding off row: Sk first bar, * **draw up lp in next bar and draw yarn through lp on hook—sl st made;** rep from * across; fasten off. With wrong side facing, whipstitch side and bottom seams.

EDGING: With C hook, join rose twist at side seam, ch 1, sc in same st. Working around top of bag, * ch 3, sc in next st, rep from * around; join with sl st to first sc; fasten off.

CORD: With rose twist and C hook, make a chain to measure 22 inches. Sl st in second ch from hook and in each ch across; fasten off. Weave cord through beading row of bag.

TASSEL (make 2): With rose twist and C hook, ch 2. Work 5 sc in second ch from hook; do not join. Mark last st and move marker at end of each rnd to mark last st. Working in back lps, work 2 sc in each sc around—10 sc.

Next 5 rnds: Sc in back lp of each st; do not join; fasten off at end of last rnd, leaving an 8-inch tail. Thread tail with tapestry needle and run gathering thread around top of tassel. Stuff tassel with fiberfill. Pull up gathering threads to close top and secure. Sew tassel to end of each cord.

For the larger bag
With afghan hook and off-white twist, ch 60.
Row 1 (first and second half): Work same as Row 1 of Smaller Bag on page 27—60 lps on hook.
Row 2 (first half): Keeping all lps on hook, sk first bar; * sk next bar, draw up lp in next bar, draw up lp in skipped bar to right; rep from * across; end draw up lp in last bar.
Row 2 (second half): Yo, draw through first lp on hook; * yo, draw through 2 lps on hook; rep from * across row until 1 lp rem on hook.
Row 3 (first half): Sk first bar, draw up lp in next bar; * sk next bar, draw up lp in next bar, draw up lp in skipped bar to right; rep from * across; end draw up lp in last 2 bars.

Row 3 (second half): Rep second half of Row 2.
Rep rows 2 and 3 until piece measures 5½ inches.
Next row (first half—beading pat): Ch 1, * draw up lp in next bar, ch 1; rep from * across; end draw up lp in last st.
Next row (second half): Rep second half of Row 2.
Rep rows 2 and 3 until piece measures 7 inches, ending with second half of either row.
Binding off row: Sk first bar, * **draw up lp in next bar and draw yarn through lp on hook—sl st made and 1 lp on hook;** rep from * across; fasten off.
With wrong side facing, whipstitch side and bottom seams.

EDGING: *Rnd 1:* Working with F hook, join teal twist at side seam, ch 1, sc in same st and in each st around; join to first sc.
Rnd 2: * Ch 4, sk sc, sc in next sc; rep from * around; end ch 2, dc in sc at beg of rnd.
Rnd 3: Sc in lp just made, * ch 4, sc in next ch-4 lp; rep from * around; end ch 4, join with sl st to first sc; fasten off.

FINISHING: With teal twist and C hook, make cord and tassel following instructions for Smaller Bag.

Sachet Pillows

Shown on page 19.

Pillows measure 5 inches square without edgings.

MATERIALS
DMC Cotton Luster Brilliant knitting and crochet cotton (50-gram ball): 1 ball *each* of yellow (No. 748), lavender (No. 210), or green (No. 955) for each pillow
Size F afghan crochet hook
Size B crochet hook
Potpourri
Old nylon stocking
Ribbons, appliqués, or other trims for embellishments

Abbreviations: See page 7.

INSTRUCTIONS
For the lavender pillow
With afghan hook and lavender thread, ch 27.
Row 1 (first half): Keeping all lps on hook, insert hook in top lp of second ch from hook, yo, draw up lp; * insert hook in top lp of next ch, yo, draw up lp; rep from * across row—27 lps on hook.
Row 1 (second half): Yo, draw through first lp on hook; * yo, draw through 2 lps on hook; rep from * across row until 1 lp rem on hook.
Row 2 (first half): Keeping all lps on hook, yo, insert hook from front to back *between* the first 2 upright bars and draw up lp, * insert hook bet the next 2 upright bars, and draw up lp, yo, draw up lp in same sp; rep from * across; end draw up lp in front of last bar and stitch behind it—79 lps on hook.
Row 2 (second half): Yo, draw through first lp on hook, * **yo, draw through 4 lps on hook—cl made;** rep from * across row—26 cls across row.
Row 3: (first half): Keeping all lps on hook, draw up lp bet first 2 cls, yo, draw up lp in same sp; * draw up lp in sp bet next 2 cls, yo, draw up lp in same sp; rep from * across row; end sk sp after last cl, draw up lp in front of last bar and st behind it—77 lps on hook.
Row 3 (second half): Yo, draw through first lp on hook; * yo, draw through 4 lps on hook; rep from * across until 2 lps rem on hook, yo, draw through 2 lps on hook—25 cls across row.
Row 4 (first half): Yo, draw up lp *bet first upright bar and first cl;* * draw up lp in sp bet next 2 cls, yo, draw up lp in same sp; rep from * across; end draw up lp in sp bet last cl and last st, yo, draw up lp in same sp, draw up lp in front of last bar and st behind it.
Row 4 (second half): Yo, draw through first lp on hook; * yo, draw through 4 lps on hook; rep from * across—26 cls.
Rep rows 3 and 4 for pat until piece is 10 inches long; fasten off.

FINISHING: With wrong sides facing, fold piece in half and sew 2 sides. Stuff an old piece of nylon stocking with potpourri and insert into pillow. Sew remaining side closed.

HEART MOTIF EDGING: With Size B crochet hook, ch 14.

Row 1: Dc in sixth ch from hook, ch 1, sk ch, dc in next 7 ch; ch 4, turn.

Row 2: Dc in fourth ch from hook, dc in next 3 dc, (ch 1, sk dc, dc in next dc) 2 times; dc in ch-1 sp, dc in next dc, ch 1, sk ch, dc in next ch; ch 4, turn.

Row 3: Sk first dc, dc in next 3 dc, (ch 1, dc in next dc) 2 times; ch 1, sk dc, dc in next 2 dc, 3 dc in top of ch-3; ch 4, turn.

Row 4: Dc in fourth ch from hook, dc in next 3 dc, ch 1, sk dc, dc in next dc, (ch 1, dc in next dc) 2 times; dc in ch-1 sp, dc in next dc, ch 1, sk dc, dc in next dc, ch 1, sk ch, dc in next ch; ch 4, turn.

Row 5: Sk first dc, dc in next dc, ch 1, dc in next dc, ch 1, sk dc, dc in next dc, dc in ch-1 sp, dc in next dc, (ch 1, dc in next dc) 2 times; ch 1, sk dc, dc in next 2 dc, 3 dc in top of ch-3; turn.

Row 6: Sk first dc, sl st in next 2 dc, ch 3, dc in next 2 dc, dc in ch-1 sp, dc in next dc, (ch 1, dc in next dc) 2 times, ch 1, sk dc, dc in next dc; dc in ch-1 sp, dc in next dc; ch 1, dc in next dc, ch 1, sk ch, dc in next ch; ch 4, turn.

Row 7: Sk first dc, dc in next dc, dc in next ch-1 sp, dc in next dc; ch 1, sk dc, dc in next dc, (ch 1, dc in next dc) 2 times; dc in ch-1 sp, dc in next 3 dc; turn.

Row 8: Sk first dc, sl st in next 2 dc, ch 3, dc in next 2 dc, dc in ch-1 sp, dc in next dc; (ch 1, dc in next dc) 2 times, dc in next 2 dc, ch 1, sk ch, dc in next ch; ch 4, turn.

Row 9: Sk first dc, dc in next dc, ch 1, sk dc, dc in next dc; (dc in next ch-1 sp, dc in next dc) 2 times; dc in next 2 dc; turn.

Row 10: Sk first dc, sl st in next 2 dc, ch 4, sk dc, dc in next dc, ch 1, sk dc, dc in next dc, ch 1, dc in next dc, ch 1, sk ch, dc in next ch; ch 4, turn.

Row 11: Sk first dc, dc in next dc, ch 1, dc in next dc, dc in ch-1 sp, dc in next dc, dc in next ch, 3 dc in next ch; ch 4, turn.

Rep rows 2–11 for pat until edging measures 28 inches or until 12 heart motifs are completed; end with Row 10; fasten off. Sew short edges together.

With same thread, run a gathering stitch around the straight edge; pull to fit around pillow. Take care to position a motif in each corner and 2 hearts along each side. Sew edging in place. Trim pillow with ribbons or appliqués as desired.

For the yellow pillow

With afghan hook and yellow thread, ch 38.

Row 1: Work same as first and second halves of Row 1 of Lavender Pillow on page 28—38 lps on hook.

Row 2 (first half): Keeping all lps on hook, sk first bar, draw up lp in each of next 3 bars; *** bring yarn to front of work and hold yarn below the row you are working in, draw up lp in each of next 3 bars—3 purl sts made;** take yarn back and draw up lp in each of next 3 bars; rep from * across; end with 3 purl sts, draw up lp in last bar and st behind it.

Row 2 (second half): Yo, draw through the first lp on the hook; * yo, draw through 2 lps on hook; rep from * across until 1 lp rem on hook.

Row 3 (first half): Sk first bar, work a purl st in each of next 2 bars, * take yarn back and draw up lp in each of next 3 bars; work a purl st in each of next 3 bars; rep from * across; ending with purl st in next to last bar, draw up lp in last bar and st behind it.

Row 3 (second half): Rep second half of Row 2.

Row 4 (first half): Sk first bar, * work a purl st in each of next 3 bars; take yarn back and draw up lp in each of next 3 bars; rep from * across; ending with yarn to back and draw up lp in last 4 bars.

Row 4 (second half): Rep second half of Row 2.

Row 5 (first half): Sk first bar, draw up lp in next bar; * work a purl st in each of next 3 sts, take

yarn back and draw up lp in each of next 3 bars; rep from * across.

Row 5 (second half): Rep second half of Row 2.

Row 6 (first half): Sk first bar, draw up lp in each of next 2 bars; * work a purl st in each of next 3 bars, take yarn back and draw up a lp in each of next 3 bars; rep from * across; ending with yarn to back, draw up lp in last 2 bars.

Row 6 (second half): Rep second half of Row 2.

Rep rows 2–6 for pat until piece is 10 inches long; fasten off.

Follow Finishing instructions for Lavender Pillow to assemble.

EDGING: With Size B crochet hook, ch 10.

Row 1: Dc in sixth ch from hook, dc in next 2 ch, ch 1, sk ch, dc in last ch; ch 5, turn.

Row 2: Dc in first dc, ch 1, dc in next 3 dc, ch 1, sk ch, dc in next ch; ch 4, turn.

Row 3: Sk first dc, dc in next dc, ch 1, sk dc, dc in next dc, dc in ch-1 sp, dc in next dc, ch 1, sk ch, dc in next ch, **ch 1, yo, draw up lp in same st as last st, yo, draw through first lp on hook, yo, (draw through 2 lps on hook)—sp-inc made;** ch 6, turn.

Row 4: Dc in fifth ch from hook, ch 1, sk ch, dc in next dc, ch 1, dc in next dc, dc in ch-1 sp, dc in next dc, ch 1, sk dc, dc in next dc, dc in ch-1 sp, dc in next dc, ch 1, sk ch, dc in next ch; ch 4, turn.

Row 5: Sk first dc, dc in next dc, ch 1, sk dc, dc in next dc, dc in ch-1 sp, dc in next dc, ch 1, sk dc, dc in next dc, ch 1, dc in next dc, dc in ch-1 sp, dc in next dc, ch 1, sk ch, dc in next ch; work sp-inc; ch 4, turn.

Row 6: Sk first dc, dc in next dc, dc in ch-1 sp, dc in next dc, ch 1, sk dc, dc in next dc; dc in ch-1 sp, dc in next dc, ch 1, dc in next dc, ch 1, sk dc, dc in next dc; ch 1, dc in next dc, ch 1, sk ch, dc in next ch; ch 4, turn.

Row 7: Sk first dc, dc in next dc, ch 1, dc in next dc, dc in ch-1 sp, dc in next dc, ch 1, dc in next dc, ch 1, sk dc, dc in next dc, dc in ch-1 sp, dc in next dc, ch 1, sk dc, dc in next dc; ch 1, sk ch, dc in next ch; turn.

continued

Row 8: Sl st in next ch and next dc, ch 4, dc in next dc, ch 1, sk dc, dc in next dc, ch 1, dc in next dc, dc in ch-1 sp, dc in next dc, ch 1, sk dc, dc in next dc, dc in ch-1 sp, dc in next dc, ch 1, sk ch, dc in next ch; ch 4, turn.

Row 9: Sk first dc, dc in next dc, ch 1, sk dc, dc in next dc, dc in ch-1 sp, dc in next dc, ch 1, sk dc, dc in next dc, ch 1, dc in next dc; turn.

Row 10: Sl st in next ch and next dc, ch 4, dc in next dc, ch 1, sk dc, dc in next dc, dc in ch-1 sp, dc in next dc, ch 1, sk ch, dc in next ch; ch 4, turn.

Row 11: Sk first dc, dc in next 3 dc, ch 1, dc in next dc; ch 5, turn.

Rep rows 2–11 eight more times; end with Row 10; fasten off. Sew short edges together.

With same thread, run a gathering stitch around the straight edge; pull to fit around pillow. Sew edging in place. Trim pillow with ribbons or appliqués.

For the green pillow

With afghan hook and green thread, ch 36.

Row 1: Work same as first and second halves of Row 1 of Lavender Pillow.

Row 2 (first half): Sk first bar, draw up lp in next bar; * **bring yarn to front of work and hold yarn below row you are working in, draw up lp in next bar—1 purl st made;** take yarn back and draw up lp in next bar; rep from * across row.

Rows 2 (second half): Yo, draw through first lp on hook; * yo, draw through 2 lps on hook; rep from * across row until 1 lp rem on hook.

Row 3 (first half): Sk first bar; * purl st in next bar, take yarn back and draw up lp in next bar; rep from * across; end draw up lps in last 2 bars.

Row 3 (second half): Rep second half of Row 2.

Rep rows 2 and 3 until piece is 10 inches long. Follow Finishing instructions for Lavender Pillow to assemble.

EDGING: With Size B crochet hook, ch 12.

Row 1: Dc in sixth ch from hook, dc in next 2 chs; (ch 1, sk ch, dc in next ch) 2 times; ch 4, turn.

Row 2: Sk first dc, dc in next dc, ch 1, dc in next 3 dc, ch 1, sk ch, dc in next ch; ch 4, turn.

Row 3: Sk first dc, dc in next dc, ch 1, sk dc, dc in next dc, dc in ch-1 sp, dc in next dc, ch 1, sk ch, dc in next ch, ch 1, **yo, draw up lp in same st as last st, yo, draw through first lp on hook, yo, (draw through 2 lps on hook)— sp-inc made;** ch 5, turn.

Row 4: Dc in first dc, ch 1, dc in next dc, dc in ch-1 sp, dc in next dc, ch 1, sk dc, dc in next dc, ch 1, dc in next dc, ch 1, sk ch, dc in next ch; ch 4, turn.

Row 5: Sk first dc, dc in next dc, (ch 1, dc in next dc) 2 times; ch 1, sk dc, dc in next dc, dc in ch-1 sp, dc in next dc, ch 1, sk ch, dc in next ch; ch 4, turn.

Row 6: Sk first dc, dc in next dc, ch 1, sk dc, dc in next dc, dc in ch-1 sp, dc in next dc, (ch 1, dc in next dc) 2 times; ch 1, sk ch, dc in next ch; ch 4, turn.

Row 7: Sk first dc, dc in next dc, ch 1, dc in next dc, dc in ch-1 sp, dc in next dc, ch 1, sk dc, dc in next dc, ch 1, dc in next dc; turn.

Row 8: Sl st in next ch and next dc, ch 4, dc in next dc, ch 1, sk dc, dc in next dc, dc in ch-1 sp, dc in next dc, ch 1, sk ch, dc in next ch; ch 4, turn.

Row 9: Sk first dc, dc in next 3 dc, ch 1, dc in next dc, ch 1, sk ch, dc in next ch; ch 4, turn.

Rep rows 2–9 twelve more times; end with Row 9; fasten off. Sew short edges together.

With same thread, run a gathering stitch around the straight edge; pull to fit around pillow. Sew edging in place. Trim pillow with ribbons or appliqués.

Flower Pillow

Shown on page 18.

Pillow measures 12½ inches square.

MATERIALS

Patons Pearl Twist (50-gram ball): 1 ball *each* of blue (No. 6098) and pale yellow (No. 6107)
Size F afghan crochet hook
Size F crochet hook
Yarn needle
14-inch square pillow form
Two 13-inch squares of matching blue fabric for pillow top and back

Abbreviations: See page 7.

INSTRUCTIONS

With blue twist and afghan crochet hook, ch 60.

Row 1 (first half): Keeping all lps on hook, insert hook in top lp of second ch from hook, yo, draw up lp; * insert hook in top lp of next ch, yo, draw up lp; rep from * across row—60 lps on hook.

Row 1 (second half): Yo, draw through first lp on hook, * yo, draw through 2 lps on hook; rep from * across row until 1 lp rem on hook.

Row 2 (first half): Keeping all lps on hook, sk first upright bar, * insert hook in next bar and draw up lp; rep from * across row—60 lps on hook.

Row 2 (second half): Yo, draw through first lp on hook, yo, draw through 2 lps on hook; * ch 3, (yo, draw through 2 lps) 2 times; rep from * across row.

Row 3 (first half): Rep first half of Row 2, taking care that all ch-3 lps of previous row fall toward front side of work to form bobble.

Row 3 (second half): Yo, draw through first lp; (yo, draw through 2 lps on hook) 2 times; * ch 3, (yo, draw through 2 lps on hook) 2 times; rep from * across row; end (yo, draw through 2 lps on hook) 3 times.

Row 4 (first half): Rep first half of Row 3.

Row 4 (second half): Rep second half of Row 2.

Row 5 (first half): Sk first bar, draw up lp in next 4 bars; * **(insert hook from front to back bet the next vertical lp bet the front and back upright bars, draw up lp—knit st made)** 21 times; draw up lp in basic afghan st in next 6 bars; rep from * 1 more time; draw up lp in basic afghan st in last 6 bars.

Row 5 (second half): Yo, draw through first lp; (yo, draw through 2 lps on hook) 2 times; * ch 3, (yo, draw through 2 lps on hook) 27 times; rep from * once more; ch 3, (yo, draw through 2 lps) 3 times.

Row 6 (first half): Rep first half of Row 5.

Row 6 (second half): Yo, draw through first lp on hook, yo, draw through 2 lps on hook; * ch 3, (yo, draw through 2 lps on hook) 2 times; ch 3, (yo, draw through 2 lps on hook) 25 times; rep from * once more; ** ch 3, (yo, draw through 2 lps on hook) 2 times; rep from ** once more.

Rows 7–27: Rep rows 5 and 6, alternately, 10 more times..

Row 28: Rep Row 5.
Row 29: Rep Row 3.
Row 30: Rep Row 2.
Row 31: Rep Row 3.
Rep rows 5–31 once more.

Last row: Sk first bar, * **draw up lp in next bar and draw yarn through lp on hook—sl st made and 1 lp on hook;** rep from * across; fasten off.

BORDER: *Rnd 1:* Join blue at any corner; with Size F crochet hook, ch 1; 3 sc in same st; sc around entire square working 3 sc in each corner; join with sl st to first sc.

Rnd 2: Sc around working 2 sc in each corner sc; join with sl st to first sc; drop blue.

Rnd 3: Join yellow in same st as join and rep Rnd 2; drop yellow.

Rnds 4 and 5: Rep Rnd 2 with blue; drop blue.

Rnd 6: Rep Rnd 2 with yellow; fasten off yellow.

Rnd 7: Rep Rnd 2 with blue.

Rnd 8: Working from left to right (reverse sc), sc in each sc around; fasten off.

CHART 1

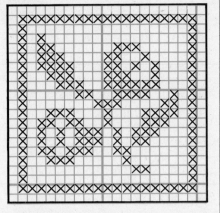

CHART 2

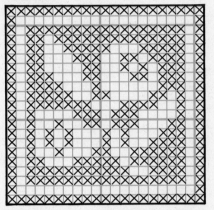

PILLOW   1 Square = 1 Stitch

COLOR KEY
⊠ **Pale Yellow**

DUPLICATE STITCH EMBROIDERY: Referring to charts 1 and 2, *above,* work duplicate stitching over the four 21-stitch blocks. See diagram, *below,* for working duplicate stitching. Referring to photo on page 18, work Chart 1 on 2 blocks, then work Chart 2 on other 2 blocks.

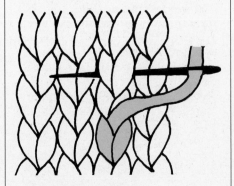

DUPLICATE STITCH

FINISHING: With right sides facing, sew 3 sides of 13-inch fabric squares together using ¼-inch seams. Insert pillow form and hand-sew fourth sides together. Pin pillow top in place and hand-sew in place.

Lacy Table Runner

Shown on page 21.

Runner measures 16x32 inches without fringe.

MATERIALS
Coats & Clark Red Heart Luster Sheen (2-ounce skein): 4 skeins of crystal pink (No. 206)
Size F aluminum afghan crochet hook
Size E aluminum crochet hook

Abbreviations: See page 7.
Gauge: 5 shells and 9 rows = 3 inches.

INSTRUCTIONS
Beg at 1 of the short edges, with afghan hook, ch 100.

Row 1 (first half): Keeping all lps on hook, insert hook in top lp of second ch from hook, yo, draw up lp, * insert hook in top lp of next ch, yo, draw up lp; rep from * across row—100 lps on hook.

Row 1: (second half): Yo, draw through 2 lps on hook, * ch 4, yo, draw through 5 lps on hook; rep from * across row until 3 lps rem on hook, ch 3, yo, draw through 3 lps, ch 1.

Row 2 (first half): Keeping all lps on hook, insert hook in top lp of first ch of the ch-3 grp, yo, draw up lp, (insert hook in top lp of next ch of the ch-3 grp, yo, draw up lp) 2 times; * insert hook in top lp of first ch of the next ch-4 grp, yo, draw up lp, (insert hook in next ch of the ch-4 grp, yo, draw up lp) 3 times; rep from * across row—100 lps on hook.

Row 2 (second half): Rep second half of Row 1.

continued

Rows 3–105: Rep Row 2. At end of second half of Row 105, change to Size E crochet hook, and sc in each ch across; fasten off.

Join thread at opposite edge of runner and sc in opposite side of foundation ch; fasten off.

FRINGE: Cut 10-inch strands of thread. * In bundles of 5, fold strands in half. With wrong side of work facing, and using crochet hook, draw folded end through sp bet shells. Pull loose ends through lp and draw tightly. Rep from * in each sp on both short ends of runner.

Colonial Star Place Mat and Coaster Set

Shown on page 20.

Place mat is 13x19 inches; coaster is 4 inches square.

MATERIALS
To make 2 place mats and 2 coasters
Red heart Luster Sheen (2-ounce skein): 4 skeins of natural (No. 805) and 1 skein of taupe (No. 332)
DMC 6-strand embroidery floss (8.7-yard skein): 3 skeins of cream (No. 712), 2 skeins *each* of antique rose (No. 224) and ice blue (No. 828)
Size 5 afghan crochet hook
Size E crochet hook
Tapestry needle

Abbreviations: See page 7.
Gauge: With Size 5 afghan hook, 14 sts and 11 rows = 2 inches.

INSTRUCTIONS
For the place mat
PANEL: With afghan hook and taupe luster sheen, ch 21.

Row 1 (first half): Keeping all lps on hook, insert hook in top lp of second ch from hook, yo, draw up lp; * insert hook in top lp of next ch, yo, draw up lp; rep from * across row—21 lps on hook.

Row 1 (second half): Yo, draw through first lp on hook; * yo, draw through 2 lps on hook; rep from * across row until 1 lp rem on hook.

Row 2 (first half): Keeping all lps on hook, sk first bar, * insert hook in next bar and draw up lp; rep from * across—21 lps on hook.

Row 2 (second half): Rep second half of Row 1.

Rows 3–68: Rep Row 2.

Row 69: Sk first bar, * **draw up lp in next bar and draw yarn through lp on hook—sl st made—1 lp on hook;** rep from * across; fasten off.

CROSS–STITCHED STARS: Referring to the chart, *above right,* cross-stitch the star motifs on the panel. Use 3 strands of floss to work the cross-stitches and French knots. Begin the first (bottom) star in the sixth row of the panel; work 1 complete motif. Skip the next 5 rows and begin to work the second star in the next row. Repeat between A–B to complete the third and fourth motifs. Five rows will remain unworked.

RIGHT SIDE: *Row 1:* With right side up, Size E crochet hook, and natural luster sheen, begin to crochet along the long side of the panel as follows: Join thread in first st under 2 lps, ch 2, sk 2 sts; * **in next st work (hdc, ch 1) 3 times, hdc in same st—shell made;** sk 3 sts; rep from * across row until 4 sts rem; end with shell, sk 2 sts, hdc in last st; ch 2, turn.

Row 2: Work shell in *center* ch-1 sp of each shell across row; end with hdc in top ch of turning ch-2; ch 2, turn.

Rows 3–40: Rep Row 2; fasten off at end of Row 40.

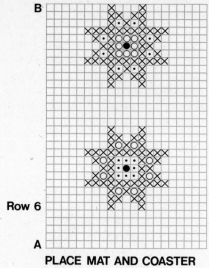

PLACE MAT AND COASTER
1 Square = 1 Stitch

COLOR KEY
⊠ **Cross-Stitch with Cream (712)**
⊡ **French Knot with Antique Rose (224)**
◯ **French Knot with Ice Blue (828)**
◉ **French Knot with Natural Luster Sheen (805)**

LEFT SIDE: Rep Right Side instructions on the opposite side of the panel for 7 rows only; fasten off.

EDGING: *Rnd 1:* With right side facing and natural luster sheen, join thread at lower right corner and work 2 sc in corner st; * sc in first ch-1 sp of shell, sl st in next ch-1 sp, sc in third ch-1 sp; hdc in sp bet shells; rep from * across side; end with sc in third ch-1 sp of last shell on side, 2 sc in corner; ** sc in each of the 2 turning chs, sc in hdc; rep from ** to panel; sc around first bar of panel; *** insert hook around next 2 bars and work sc; sc around next bar; rep from *** across panel sts only; rep bet ** to corner; 2 sc in corner; work rem 2 sides to correspond; join with sl st to first sc.

Rnds 2 and 3: Work reverse sc (sc from left to right) in each st around; join with sl st to first sc; at end of Rnd 3, fasten off.

For the coaster

With taupe luster sheen and afghan hook, ch 19.

Rep rows 1 and 2 of place mat panel—19 lps on hook at end of first half of every row.

Rows 3-19: Rep Row 2.

Row 20: Rep Row 69 of place mat panel.

Work cross-stitching following chart, *opposite*.

BORDER (right side): *Row 1:* With right side facing, Size E hook, and natural luster sheen, work along side of panel as follows: Join thread in first st, ch 2, sk st, * work shell in next st, sk 3 sts; rep from * across side; end hdc in last edge st; ch 2, turn.

Row 2: Work shell in center ch-1 sp of *each* shell across; end with hdc in top of ch-2; fasten off.

Rep rows 1 and 2 on opposite side of coaster square.

EDGING: Work same as place mat edging on page 30.

Aran Hat, Scarf And Mitten Set

Shown on pages 22-23.

Directions are for size Medium. Changes for child's size Large and man's size Medium are in parentheses. Mittens fit hand measurements of 5-5½ (6-6½, 8-9) inches. Hat fits crown measurements of 20 (21, 23) inches. Scarf measures 7x36 (8x55) inches, less fringe.

MATERIALS

Bernat Berella Sport Spun (50-gram ball): 5 (6, 8) balls of sandstone heather (No. 2892) for child's; walnut heather (No. 2816) for man's

Sizes 8, 9, and 10.5 afghan crochet hooks

Size F crochet hook

Stitch holder

Abbreviations: See page 7.

Gauge: With 10.5 afghan hook, 9 sts and 9 rows of afghan crochet knit sts = 2 inches.

INSTRUCTION
For the scarf

With Size 10.5 afghan hook, ch 33 (37).

Row 1 (first half): Keeping all lps on hook, insert hook in top lp of second ch from hook, yo, draw up lp, * insert hook in top lp of next ch, yo, draw up lp; rep from * across row—33 (37) lps on hook.

Row 1: (second half): Yo, draw through first lp on hook, * yo, draw through 2 lps on hook; rep from * across row until 1 lp rem on hook.

Row 2 (first half): Sk first up-right bar, * **insert hook, from front, through center of next vertical lp, to the back of the work, yo, draw up lp—k st made;** rep from * across—33 (37) lps on hook.

Row 2 (second half and all subsequent second halves of rows): Rep second half of Row 1.

Rows 3-5: Rep Row 2.

Row 6: Sk first bar, k 2 (3), * k 1, sk next 3 sts; **trc around the third st below (Row 3) the last skipped st—ltr made;** k 1 in next st of Row 6; trc around the same st as first ltr; k 3, (k 1, trc around the same st as first ltr) twice; k 3, rep from * 2 times more; end k 4 on large size only—33 (37) lps on hook.

Rows 7 and 8: Rep Row 2.

Row 9: Sk first st; k 5 (6), **holding back last lp of each trc, trc around post of first and then second ltr below; k 1, holding back last lp of each trc, trc around post of third and then fourth ltr below; yo, draw through 5 lps on hook—trc-cl made;** k 7 (8), (trc around ltr below, k 1) 2 times; k 3 more sts, (trc around next ltr, k 1) 2 times; k 5 (6); work trc-cl; end k 6 (7).

Rows 10 and 11: Rep Row 2.

Row 12: Sk first st, k 3, (4); * (trc around all sts of trc-cl below, k 1) 2 times; k 3; rep from * once more; k 2 more sts, work trc-cl; k 7; rep bet *s twice more; end k 2 (3).

Rows 13 and 14: Rep Row 2.

Row 15: Sk first st, k 5 (6), work trc-cl; k 7 (8), (trc around trc-cl, k 1) 2 times; k 3 more sts; (trc around trc-cl, k 1) 2 times; k 5 more sts; work trc-cl; end k 6 (7).

Rows 16 and 17: Rep Row 2.

Row 18: Sk first st, k 3 (4), * (trc around all sts of trc-cl below, k 1) 2 times; k 3 more sts; rep from * once more; k 3 (4) more sts, (trc around next ltr, k 1) twice; k 3; (trc around next ltr, k 1) twice; k 3 (k 4) more sts, rep bet *s 2 times; end k 4 on large size only.

Rows 19 and 20: Rep Row 2.

Row 21: Sk first st, k 5 (6), * working in succession in each of the ltr posts below, work trc-cl; k 9 (10), rep from * twice more; end k 6 (7) instead of k 9 (10).

Rows 22 and 23: Rep Row 2.

Rep rows 6–23 for pat 7 (12) times more; in Row 6 when working ltrs, insert hook under all post sts; fasten off.

With Size F crochet hook, work 1 row of sc into each long side of scarf. Work 1 row of sc and 1 row of reverse sc (crochet from left to right) into each short end of scarf. Cut 10- (12-) inch strands of yarn for fringe. In bundles of 5, knot fringe into every third sc on both short ends.

For the mittens

RIGHT MITTEN: With Size 9 afghan hook, ch 31 (35, 41). Rep Row 1 of Scarf.

Row 2 (ribbing): Sk first st, * k 2, p 1; rep from * across row; end k 3, (3, 1).

Rows 3–11: Rep Row 2. At end of Row 11, change to Size 10.5 hook and beg palm.

HAND: *Row 1* (child's sizes only): Sk first st, k 31 (35).

(Man's size only): K 20, **insert hook bet vertical lps, from front to back of work, yo, draw up lp—inc made;** k 1, inc 1, k 20—43 sts.

Rows 2 and 3: Sk first st, k all rem sts.

continued

Row 4: Sk first st, k 5 (6, 8); sk next 3 sts; **trc around the third st below (Row 1) the last skipped st—ltr made;** k 1 in next st of Row 4; trc around the same st as first ltr; k 3; * k 1, trc around the same st as first ltr; k 3, rep from * 2 more times; end k 16 (19, 25).

Rows 5 and 6: Sk first st, k 31 (35, 43).

Row 7: Sk first st, k 7, (8, 10); **holding back last lp of each trc, trc around post of first and then second ltr below; k 1, holding back last lp of each trc, trc around post of third and then fourth ltr below; yo, draw through 5 lps on hook—trc-cl made;** end k 22 (25, 31).

Rows 8 and 9: Sk first st, k all sts.

For child's size Medium only
THUMB OPENING: *Row 10:* Sk first st, k 5, * (trc around all sts of trc-cl below, k 1) 2 times; k 3; rep from * once more; k 2 more, work off as for second half of row, sl first lp on hook to holder, sk next 4 sts at end of first half of row just worked; with separate strand of yarn, rejoin in next st with k st; k next 8 sts; work off sts, ch 4; fasten off.

Row 11: Sk first st, k 17, draw up lp in each of next 4 chs, k 9.

Row 12: K all sts.

Row 13: Rep Row 7.

Rows 14 and 15: K all sts.

Rows 16–25: Rep rows 4–9, ending with Row 7.

Row 26: Sk first st, k 1, **insert hook, knitwise, into each of next sts, yo draw up lp—k 2 tog made;** k 8, k 2 tog, k 3, k 2 tog, k 8, k 2 tog; k 2.

Row 27: Sk first st, k 1, k 2 tog, k 6, k 2 tog, k 3; k 2 tog, k 6, k 2 tog; k 2.

Row 28: Sk first st, k 1, k 2 tog, (k 1, trc under all sts of trc-cl) 2 times; k 2, k 2 tog, k 1, trc around all sts of trc-cl; k 3, k 2 tog, k 4, k 2 tog, k 2.

Row 29: Sk first st, k 1, k 2 tog, k 2, k 2 tog, k 3, k 2 tog, k 2, k 2 tog, k 2.

Row 30 (first half): Knit all sts.
Row 30 (second half): Yo, draw through all lps on hook, cut yarn; fasten off.

For child's size Large only
Row 10: Rep Row 4, working ltrs under all sts of trc-cl.
Row 11: K all sts.

THUMB OPENING: *Row 12:* Sk first st, k 19, work off as for second half of row. Sl lp on hook to holder, sk 4 sts at end of first half of row just worked; with separate strand of yarn, rejoin in next st with k st; ; join separate strand of yarn in fifth st, k 10, work off as for second half of row, ch 4; fasten off.

Row 13: Sk first st, k 9, work trc-cl, k 10, draw up lp in each of next 4 chs, k 11.

Rows 14 and 15: K all sts.

Rows 16–28: Rep rows 4–9, ending with Row 4.

Row 29: Sk first st, k 1, **insert hook, knitwise, into each of next sts, yo draw up lp—k 2 tog made;** k 10, k 2 tog, k 3, k 2 tog, k 10, k 2 tog, k 2.

Row 30: Sk first st, k 1, k 2 tog, k 8, k 2 tog, k 3, k 2 tog, k 8, k 2 tog, k 2.

Row 31: Sk first st, k 1, k 2 tog, k 3, work trc-cl, k 2, k 2 tog, k 3, k 2 tog, k 6, k 2 tog, k 2.

Row 32: Sk first st, k 1, k 2 tog, k 4, k 2 tog, k 3, k 2 tog, k 4, k 2 tog, k 2.

Row 33: Sk first st, k 1, k 2 tog, k 2, k 2 tog, k 3, k 2 tog, k 2, k 2 tog, k 2.

Row 34 (first half): Knit all sts.
Row 34 (second half): Yo, draw through all lps on hook, cut yarn; fasten off.

For man's size only
Row 10: Rep Row 4, working ltrs under all sts of trc-cl.
Rows 11 and 12: K all sts.
Row 13: Rep Row 7.
Rows 14 and 15: K all sts.
Row 16: Rep Row 4.
Row 17: K all sts.

THUMB OPENING: *Row 18:* Sk first st, k 23, work off lps as for second half of row, sl lp on hook to holder; sk 6 sts at end of first half of row just worked, join separate strand of yarn in next st with k st, k 12, work off lps as for second half of row, ch 6; fasten off.

Row 19: Sk first st, k 10, work trc-cl, k 12, draw up lp in each of next 6 chs, k 13.

Rows 20 and 21: K all sts.

Rows 22–37: Rep rows 4–9, ending with Row 7.

Row 38: Sk first st, k 1, k 2 tog, k 14, k 2 tog, k 3, k 2 tog, k 12, k 2 tog, k 2.

Row 39: Sk first st, k 1, k 2 tog, k 12, k 2 tog, k 3, k 2 tog, k 12, k 2 tog, k 2.

Row 40: Sk first st, k 1, k 2 tog, k 2, (k 1, trc under all sts of trc-cl) 2 times; k 3, rep bet ( )s twice more; k 1, k 2 tog, k 3, k 2 tog, k 10, k 2 tog, k 2.

Row 41: Sk first st, k 1, k 2 tog, k 8, k 2 tog, k 3, k 2 tog, k 8, k 2 tog, k 2.

Row 42: Sk first st, k 1, k 2 tog, k 6, k 2 tog, k 3, k 2 tog, k 6, k 2 tog, k 2.

Row 43: Sk first st, k 1, k 2 tog, k 2, work trc-cl, k 1, k 2 tog, k 3, k 2 tog, k 4, k 2 tog, k 2.

Row 44 (first half): Knit all sts.
Row 44 (second half): Yo, draw through all lps on hook, cut yarn; fasten off.

For all sizes
THUMB: *Row 1:* Insert hook, knitwise, into st beside bottom right of thumb opening, yo, draw up lp, draw up lp in each of 4 (4, 6) skipped sts in Row 10 (12, 18), draw up lp at left side of thumb opening—6 (6, 8) sts.

Rows 2–10 (2–12, 2–16): Knit all sts.

Rows 11 and 13 for child's sizes only: Sk first st, k 2 tog, k 2 tog, k 1.

Rows 12 and 14: Sk first st, k 2 tog, k 1; fasten off.

Row 17 for man's size: Sk first st, (k 2 tog) 3 times; k 1.

Row 18: Sk first st, k 2 tog, k 2; fasten off.

Turn work in opposite direction (cuff side up) and work into opposite side of thumb opening in same manner as for first. With crochet hook and right sides facing, sl st sides of thumb tog. With right sides facing, sl st sides of mittens tog.

LEFT MITTEN: Work as for Right Mitten, reversing shaping.

For the hat
With Size 8 afghan hook, ch 107 (111, 119).
Rep Row 1 of Scarf.
Row 2 (ribbing): Sk first st, * k 3, p 1; rep from * across row; end k 3.
Rows 3–7 (3–7, 3–10): Rep Row 2. At end of Row 7 (7, 10), change to 10.5 hook.

CROWN: *Row 1:* Sk first st, k all sts.
Rows 2 and 3: Rep Row 1 of Crown.
Row 4: Sk first st, k 40, (42, 46), * sk next 3 sts; **trc around the third st below (Row 1) the last skipped st—ltr made;** k 1, trc around same st below, k 3; (k 1, trc around same st below) 2 times; k 4, rep from * twice more; end k 36 (38, 42) more.
Rows 5 and 6: K all sts.
Row 7: Sk first st, k 42, (44, 48), **holding back last lp of each trc, trc around post of first and then second ltr below; k 1, holding back last lp of each trc, trc around post of third and then fourth ltr below; yo, draw through 5 lps on hook—trc-cl made;** k 7, trc around ltr below, k 1, trc around next ltr below; k 4, trc around next ltr below, k 1, trc around next ltr below; k 6, work trc-cl, k 43 (45, 49).
Rows 8 and 9: K all sts.
Row 10: Sk first st, k 40 (42, 46); * (trc under all sts of trc-cl, k 1) 2 times; k 3 more; rep from * once more; k 2 more, work trc-cl, k 7, (trc under all sts of trc-cl, k 1) 2 times; k 3 more; rep bet ( )s twice; k 39 (41, 45).
Rows 11 and 12: K all sts.

Row 13: Sk first st, k 42, (44, 48); work trc-cl; k 7, trc around ltr, k 1, trc around next ltr; k 4, trc around next ltr, k 1, trc around next ltr; k 6, work trc-cl, k 43 (45, 49).
Rows 14 and 15: K all sts.
Row 16: Sk first st, k 40 (42, 46), (trc around all sts of trc-cl, k 1) 2 times; k 3, (trc around all sts of trc-cl, k 1) 2 times; k 3, trc around ltr, k 1, trc around next ltr; k 4, trc around next ltr, k 1, trc around next ltr; k 4, (trc around all sts of trc-cl, k 1) 2 times, k 3, (trc around all sts of trc-cl, k 1) 2 times; end k 39 (41, 45).
Row 17 and 18: K all sts.
Row 19: Sk first st, k 42 (44, 48), work trc-cl, (k 9, work trc-cl) twice; k 43 (45, 49).
Row 20: K all sts.
Row 21: Sk first st, k 2 (0, 2), k 2 tog, (k 2, k 2 tog) 9 (10, 10) times; k 25 (25, 29), k 2 tog; (k 2, k 2 tog) 9 (10, 10) times; end k 3 (1, 3).
Row 22: Sk first st, k 30 (31, 35); * (trc around all sts of trc-cl, k 1) 2 times; k 3, (trc around all sts of trc-cl, k 1) 2 times; k 3; rep from * 2 more times; k 26, (27, 34).
Row 23: Sk first st, k 1, (1, 2), k 2 tog, (k 2, k 2 tog) 6 (6, 7) times; k 8 (9, 8); k 2 tog, k 1, k 2 tog, k 5, k 2 tog, k 1, k 2 tog, k 8 (9, 8), k 2 tog, (k 2, k 2 tog) 6 (6, 7) times; end k 2 (2, 3).
Row 24: K all sts.
Row 25: Sk first st, k 1 (0, 1); k 2 tog, (k 1, k 2 tog) 7 (8, 8) times; k 1 (0, 2), work trc-cl; k 1 (1, 2), k 2 tog, k 2 (2, 1), trc around ltr, k 1, trc around next ltr; k 4, trc around next ltr, k 1, trc around next ltr; k 1 (1, 0), k 2 tog, k 1, (1, 2); work trc-cl; k 1 (0, 2), k 2 tog, (k 1, k 2 tog) 7 (8, 8) times; k 2 (1, 2).
Row 26: K all sts.
Row 27: Sk first st, k 1, k 2 tog; (k 1, k 2 tog) 4 (4, 5) times; k 5; (k 2 tog) 2 (2, 1) times; k 1, (1, 5); (k 2 tog) 2 (2, 1) times; k 5, k 2 tog; (k 1, k 2 tog) 4 (4, 5) times; k 2.

For child's size only
Row 28: Sk first st, (k 2 tog) 5 times; (k 1, trc around all sts of trc-cl) 2 times; k 1, (k 1, trc around all sts of trc-cl) 2 times; k 2 tog, work trc-cl; k 2 tog, (k 1, trc around all sts of trc-cl) 2 times; k 1, (k 1, trc around all sts of trc-cl) 2 times; (k 2 tog) 5 times; k 1.
Row 29 (first half): Sk first st, k 2 tog, k 1, k 2 tog, k 13, (k 2 tog, k 1) 2 times.
Row 29 (second half): Yo, draw through all lps on hook, cut yarn, draw yarn through last lp on hook.

For man's size only
Row 28: Sk first st, k 12, (k 1, trc around all sts of trc-cl,) 2 times; k 1, (k 1, trc around all sts of trc-cl) 2 times; k 3, work trc-cl, k 3; (k 1, trc around all sts of trc-cl,) 2 times; k 1, (k 1, trc around all sts of trc-cl) 2 times; k 13.
Row 29: Sk first st, * k 2 tog; rep from * across row; end k 2.
Row 30: K all sts.
Row 31: Rep Row 29.
Row 32 (first half): K all sts.
Row 32 (second half): Yo, draw through all lps on hook, fasten off.

FINISHING: With Size F hook and right sides facing, sl st back seam of hat together. With right side facing, work 1 row of sc around bottom edge of hat; join with sl st to first sc; do not turn. Work 1 row of reverse sc (work from left to right) around; join with sl st to first sc; fasten off.

EXCEPTIONAL GIFTS

Heart Motif Hat, Scarf, and Mitten Set

Shown on pages 22–23.

Directions are for child's size Medium. Changes for child's size Large and woman's size are in parentheses. Mittens fit hand measurements of 5–5½ (6–6½, 7–8) inches. Hat fits crown measurements of 20 (21, 22) inches. Scarf measures 7x36 (8x48) inches, less fringe.

MATERIALS
Bernat Berella Sportspun (50-gram ball): 4 (4, 5) balls MC; 1 ball *each* of colors A and B for all sizes
For child, MC is denim heather (No. 2866), A is marsh heather (No. 2852), and B is natural (No. 2859)
For woman, MC is cranberry (No. 2838), A is navy (No. 2865), and B is natural (No. 2859)
Sizes 8, 9, and 10.5 afghan crochet hooks
Size F crochet hook
Stitch holder

Abbreviations: See page 7.
Gauge: With 10.5 afghan hook, 9 afghan sts and 9 rows = 2 inches.

INSTRUCTIONS
For the scarf
With MC and 10.5 afghan hook, ch 33 (40).
Row 1 (first half): Keeping all lps on hook, insert hook in top lp of second ch from hook, yo, draw up lp, * insert hook in top lp of next ch, yo, draw up lp; rep from * across row—33 (40) lps on hook.
Row 1: (second half): Yo, draw through first lp on hook, * yo, draw through 2 lps on hook; rep from * across row until 1 lp rem on hook.
Row 2 (first half): Sk first upright bar, * **insert hook from front, through center of next vertical lp, to back of work, yo, draw up lp—k st made;** rep from * across row—33 (40) lps on hook.
Row 2 (second half): Rep second half of Row 1.
Rows 3–16 (21): Rep Row 2; at end of second half of Row 16 (21), draw through last 2 lps with A.
Row 17 (22): With A, rep Row 2; draw through last 2 lps with B.
Rows 18 and 19 (23–26): With B, rep Row 2.
Note: Work the heart motifs in the next 4 rows. Cut 4 yarn strands, each 2 yards long, and work each heart with separate strand of yarn. Carry B yarn across back of work. Always carry the color not in use along the back of work. To avoid long strands, cross strand of yarn not in use over strand of yarn that is in use every second or third stitch.
When working the second half of the row, draw through each lp with the same color used for the matching st in the first half of the row, dropping colors to the back of the work and stranding in the same manner as for the first half of the row.
Row 20 (27): Sk first st, with B, k 6 (5) sts; with A, k 1 st; * with B, k 8 sts; with A, k 1 st; rep from * across row; end k 7 (6) with B.
Row 21 (28): Sk first st, with B, k 5 (4); k 3 with A; * k 6 with B; k 3 with A; rep from * across row; end k 6 (5) with B.
Row 22 (29): Sk first st, k 4 (3) with B, k 5 with A; * k 4 with B; k 5 with A; rep from * across row; end k 5 (4) with B.
Row 23 (30): Sk first st, k 4 (3) with B; k 2 with A, k 1 with B; k 2 with A; * k 4 with B; k 2 with A, k 1, with B; k 2 with A; rep from * across row; end k 5 (4) with B.
Rows 24 and 25 (31–34): Rep rows 18 and 19 (23–26).
Row 26 (35): Rep Row 17 (22), changing to MC at end of row.
Rep Row 2 until piece measures 30 (40) inches from beg.
Work rows 2–26 in reverse order to mirror the first side; at end of Row 26, fasten off.

FINISHING: Using Size F crochet hook, sc evenly spaced along each long side, working the same number of sts on each side. Work 1 row of sc and 1 row of reverse sc (crochet from left to right) along each short end of scarf.
Cut 10-inch (12-inch) strands of yarn. In bundles of 5, knot fringe in every third sc along short edges of scarf.

For the hat
With Size 8 afghan hook and MC, ch 107 (112, 117).
Row 1: Rep Row 1 of Scarf.
Row 2 (begin ribbing): * K 3, **bring yarn to front of work, insert hook from back to front through center of next vertical lp, yo, draw up lp—p st made;** rep from * across; end k 3 (4, 1).
Row 2 (second half): Rep second half of Row 1 of Scarf.
Rows 3–7: Rep Row 2. At end of Row 7, change to Size 10.5 hook and begin to work crown.

CROWN: *Row 1:* Sk first st, with MC, k 106 (111, 116).
Rows 2 and 3: Rep Row 1 of Crown. Change to A at end of second half of Row 3.
Row 4: With A, k all sts; change to B at end of second half of row.
Rows 5 and 6: With B, k all sts.
Row 7: Sk first st, k 3 (5, 3) with B, k 1 with A; * k 8 with B, k 1 with A; rep from * across row; end k 3 (6, 4) with B.
Row 8: Sk first st, k 2 (4, 2) with B, k 3 with A; * k 6 with B, k 3 with A; rep from * across row; end k 2 (5, 3) with B.
Row 9: Sk first st, k 1 (3, 1) with B, k 5 with A; * k 4 with B, k 5 with A; rep from * across row; end k 1, (4, 2) with B.
Row 10: Sk first st, k 1 (3, 1) with B; k 2 with A, k 1 with B, k 2 with A; * k 4 with B, k 2 with A, k 1 with B, k 2 with A; rep from * across row; end k 1 (4, 2) with B.
Rows 11 and 12: Rep rows 5 and 6.
Row 13: Rep Row 4.
Rows 14–21 (14–21, 14–26): With MC, k all sts.

Row 22 (22–27): Sk first st, k 1, *** insert hook through center of next 2 vertical lps, yo, draw through the 2 lps—k 2 tog (dec made);** k 2; rep from * across; end k 3, (4, 1).

Row 23 (23–28): K all sts.

Row 24 (24–29): Sk first st, * k 2 tog, k 1; rep from * across; end k 3, (1, 1).

Row 25 (25–30): K all sts.

Row 26 (26–31): Rep Row 24; end k 2.

Rows 27 and 28 (27–28, 32–33): Rep rows 25 and 26 (25–26, 30–31).

Row 29 (29–34), (first half): K all sts.

Row 29 (second half): Yo, draw through all lps on hook; fasten off leaving 8-inch end; yo, draw through rem lp on hook.

FINISHING: With Size F crochet hook, MC, and right sides facing, sl st back seams of hat tog.

With right side facing, work 1 rnd sc around bottom edge of hat; join with sl st to first sc; ch 1, do not turn. Work 1 rnd reverse sc (crochet from left to right); join to first sc; fasten off. Weave in ends.

For the mittens

RIGHT MITTEN: Beg at cuff edge, with Size 9 afghan hook and MC, ch 31 (35, 37).

Row 1: Rep Row 1 of Scarf.

Row 2 (begin ribbing): *** K 3, bring yarn to front of work, insert hook from back through center of next vertical lp to the front of the work, yo, draw up lp—p st made;** rep from * across, end with k 3 (3, 1).

Row 2 (second half): Rep second half of Row 1 of Scarf.

Rows 3–11: Rep Row 2. At end of Row 11, change to size 10.5 afghan hook to begin hand.

For child's sizes only

HAND: *Row 1:* With MC, k all sts.

For woman's size only

Row 1: Sk first st, with MC, k 17, **insert hook, from front, *between* next 2 vertical lps, to back of work and draw up a lp—inc made;** k 1, inc 1; k 18—39 sts.

For all sizes

Rows 2–5 (2–7, 2–8): K all sts.

Row 6 (8, 9): Sk first st, k 7 (8, 9) with MC, k 1 with A, k 22 (25, 28) with MC.

Row 7 (9, 10): Sk first st, k 6 (7, 8) with MC, k 3 with A, k 21 (24, 27) with MC.

Row 8 (10, 11): Sk first st, k 5 (6, 7) with MC, k 5 with A, k 20 (23, 26) with MC.

Row 9 (11, 12): Sk first st, k 5 (6, 7) with MC, k 2 with A, k 1 with MC, k 2 with A, k 20 (23, 26) with MC.

For woman's size only

Rows 13–15: With MC, k all sts.

For all sizes

Row 10, (12, 16): Sk first st, with MC, k 17 (19, 21). Work second half of row over these sts on the hook; sl last lp onto st holder; sk next 4 (4, 5) sts at end of first half of row just completed; join yarn in next st as if to k; k 8 (10, 11); work second half of row over these sts; ch 4 (4, 5); fasten off—thumb opening established.

For child's sizes only

Row 11 (13): Sk first st, with MC, k 17 (19), draw up lp in each of the 4 chs, k 9 (11).

Rows 12 and 13 (14–15): K all 31 (35) sts.

Row 14 (16): Rep Row 6 (8).

For woman's size only

Row 17: Sk first st, k 9 with MC; k 1 with A, k 11 with MC; with MC, draw up lps in each of next 5 chs, k 12 with MC.

For all sizes

Rows 15–17 (17–19, 18–20): Rep rows 7–9 (9–11, 10–12).

Rows 18–21 (20–23, 21–24): K all 31 (35, 39) sts with MC.

Rows 22–25 (24–27 25–28): Rep rows 6–9 (8–11, 9–12).

Note: Work all subsequent rows with MC.

For child's size Large and woman's size

Row 28 (29–31): K 35 (39) sts.

For woman's size only

Row 32: Sk first st, k 1, *** insert hook through center of next 2 vertical lps, yo, draw through the 2 lps—k 2 tog (dec made);** k 12, k 2 tog, k 3, k 2 tog, k 12, k 2 tog, k 2.

For child's size Large and woman's size

Row 29 (33): Sk first st, k 1, k 2 tog, k 10, k 2 tog, k 3, k 2 tog, k 10, k 2 tog, k 2.

For all sizes

Row 26 (30, 34): Sk first st, k 1, k 2 tog, k 8, k 2 tog, k 3, k 2 tog, k 8, k 2 tog, k 2.

Row 27 (31, 35): Sk first st, k 1, k 2 tog, k 6, k 2 tog, k 3, k 2 tog, k 6, k 2 tog, k 2.

Row 28 (32, 36): Sk first st, k 1, k 2 tog, k 4, k 2 tog, k 3, k 2 tog, k 4, k 2 tog, k 2.

Row 29 (33, 37): Sk first st, k 1, k 2 tog, k 2, k 2 tog, k 3, k 2 tog, k 2, k 2 tog, k 2.

Row 30 (34, 38) (first half): K all sts.

Row 30 (34, 38) (second half): Yo, draw through all lps on hook—1 lp on hook. Cut yarn, leaving sufficient length to secure; draw yarn end through rem lp on hook.

THUMB: *Row 1:* Insert hook into st beside bottom right of thumb opening (as for k), yo, draw up lp; draw up lp in each of the 4 (4, 5) sts skipped in Row 10 (12, 16); draw up lp at left side of thumb opening—6 (6, 7) sts.

Rows 2–10 (2–12, 2–14): K all sts across row.

For child's sizes only

Row 11 (13): Sk first st, (k 2 tog) 2 times; k 1.

Row 12 (14): Sk first st, k 2 tog, k 1; fasten off.

For woman's size only

Row 15: Sk first st, k 2 tog, k 1, k 2 tog, k 1.

Row 16: Sk first st, (k 2 tog) 2 times; fasten off.

FINISHING: Turn work with cuff side up and work into other side of thumb opening in same

continued

manner as for first side. Push thumb sides through to wrong side. With MC and Size F crochet hook, sl st thumb sides tog. Secure and trim loose ends.

With right sides facing, crochet mitten sides tog in same manner.

For woman's size only
With MC and Size F hook, work 1 rnd sc around bottom edge of cuff; join with sl st to first sc; do not turn. Ch 1, work 1 rnd of reverse sc (work from left to right); join with sl st to first sc; fasten off.

LEFT MITTEN: Repeat Right Mitten through Row 5 (7, 8).
Row 6 (8, 9): Sk first st, k 21 (24, 27) with MC, k 1 with A, k 8 (9, 10) with MC.
Row 7 (9, 10): Sk first st, k 20 (23, 26) with MC, k 3 with A, k 7 (8, 9) with MC.
Row 8 (10, 11): Sk first st, k 19 (22, 25) with MC, k 5 with A, k 6 (7, 8) with MC.
Row 9 (11, 12): Sk first st, k 19 (22, 25) with MC, k 2 with A, k 1 with MC, k 2 with A, k 6 (7, 8) with MC.

For woman's size only
Rows 13-15: With MC, knit all sts across row.

All sizes
Row 10 (12, 16): Sk first st, with MC, k 8 (10, 11), Work second half of row over all sts on hook; sl last lp onto st holder; sk next 4 (4, 5) sts; join separate strand of yarn in next st as if to knit, k 17 (19, 21), ch 4 (4, 5); fasten off.

For child's sizes only
Row 11 (13): Sk first st, with MC, k 8 (10), draw up lps in each of next 4 chs, k 18 (20).

For woman's size only
Row 17: Sk first st, k 11 with MC, draw up lps in each of next 5 chs, k 11 with MC, k 1 with A, k 10 with MC.
Rows 12-30 (14-34, 18-38): Work as for Right Mitten, except work heart pat rows 6-9 (8-11, 9-12).

Woman's Pullovers

Shown on pages 24–25.

Directions are for size Small. Changes for sizes Medium and Large follow in parentheses. Finished bust = 34 (37, 40) inches.

MATERIALS
Worsted-weight yarn (3.5-ounce skein): 7 (8, 8) skeins of pink or blue; scraps of assorted colors for cross-stitch
Size G afghan crochet hook
Size G crochet hook
Yarn needle

Abbreviations: See page 7.
Gauge: Over afghan stitch, 4 sts = 1 inch; 7 rows = 2 inches

INSTRUCTIONS
For the boat-neck pullover
BACK WAISTBAND: With crochet hook, ch 15; turn.
Row 1: Sl st in second ch from hook and in each rem ch across—14 sts; ch 1, turn.
Row 2: Sl st in back lp of each sl st across; ch 1, turn.
Rep Row 2 until there is a total of 68 (74, 80) rows or 34 (37, 40) ridges; do not fasten off.

BODY: *Row 1* (first half): Transfer lp on hook to afghan hook; working along edge of waistband, pick up 1 lp in each row across—69 (75, 81) lps on hook.
Row 1 (second half): Yo, draw through first lp on hook; * yo, draw through 2 lps on hook; rep from * across row until 1 lp rem on hook.
Row 2 (first half): Keeping all lps on hook, sk first bar, * insert hook in next bar and draw up lp; rep from * across—69 (75, 81) lps on hook.
Row 2 (second half): Rep second half of Row 1.
Rows 3–40 (43, 46): Rep Row 2.

ARMHOLE SHAPING: Sk first bar, * **draw up lp in next bar and draw yarn through lp on hook— sl st made;** rep from * 4 (6, 8) more times; draw up lp under next 58 (60, 62) bars. With separate length of yarn, and regular crochet hook, sl st across last 5 (7, 9) sts—58 (60, 62) sts on hook.
Sk first bar, **insert hook under next 2 bars, yo, draw yarn through both bars—dec made;** draw up bars in each st across row until 3 bars rem; dec over next 2 bars, draw up lp in last bar; complete second half of row as usual. Rep this row twice more—52 (54, 56) sts. Work even until 20 (22, 24) rows are completed past beg of armhole.

NECK SHAPING: Sl st across 10 (12, 14) sts at each end of next row as for armhole shaping; complete second half of row—32 (30, 28) sts.

NECK FACING: *Next row:* **Insert hook in sp between next 2 bars, yo, draw up lp—inc made;** draw up lp in next bar; draw up lp in each bar across until 1 bar rem; work inc, draw up lp in last bar; complete second half of row—34 (32, 30) sts. Work even for 1 row.
Next row: Inc 1 st at each end of row—36 (34, 32) sts; complete second half of row. Sl st across row; fasten off.

FRONT: Work as for Back.

SLEEVES: *For wristband,* work ribbing as for Back until there is a total of 44 (46, 48) rows or 22 (23, 24) ridges.
Working along edge of wristband, draw up 44 (46, 48) lps on hook. Work even in basic afghan st for 10 rows.
Inc 1 st at beg and end of next row. Inc every 10th row until there is a total of 50 (52, 54) lps on hook. Work even until there is a total of 40 (43, 46) rows. Sl st across 5 (7, 9) sts at each side as for armhole shaping. Dec 1 st at each end of row until 12 sts rem. Sl st across row; fasten off.

CROSS-STITCHING: Referring to photograph and following chart, *bottom right*, cross-stitch design on sweater front.

FINISHING: All seaming is done on right side of sweater. With wrong sides together, join shoulder seams, including neck facing. Center sleeve cap at shoulder seam. Sl st sleeve to armhole. Beg at wrist, sl st sleeve and side seam. Fold neck facing to inside and stitch in place.

For the crewneck pullover

BACK: Work as for boat-neck pullover, omitting neck facing. Sl st across all sts; fasten off.

FRONT: Work as for Back until 12 (13, 14) rows are completed past beg of armhole shaping.

NECK SHAPING: Work over first 16 (17, 18) sts. Leaving these lps on needle, with separate ball of yarn sl st across center 20 sts— 16 (17, 18) lps rem on each side.

Working on left side of neck only, dec 1 st at neck edge 3 times—13 (14, 15) sts. Work even until total of 20 (22, 24) rows are completed past beg of neck shaping. Sl st across sts of right shoulder. Join thread at left side of center neck sts and complete second half of row on 16 (17, 18) sts of left shoulder. Work as for first side of neck, reversing shaping.

SLEEVES: Work as for Boat-Neck Pullover.

Join seams as for Boat-Neck Pullover.

NECKBAND: Ch 7. Work as for Back waist ribbing having 6 sts, until there is a total of 72 (76, 80) rows or 36 (38, 40) ridges. Sl st ends together, forming ring. With wrong sides tog and seam of neckband at shoulder seam, sl st neckband around neck edge.

CROSS-STITCHING: Referring to photograph and following chart, *top right*, cross-stitch design on sweater front.

BOAT-NECK PULLOVER

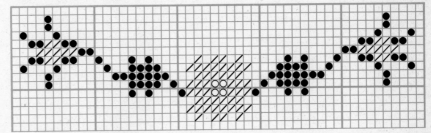

CREWNECK PULLOVER   **1 Square = 1 Cross-Stitch**

COLOR KEY

- ● Green   ☒ Blue
- ○ Yellow   ◲ Pink

DESIGNS FOR KIDS

FULL OF SPUNK AND SPIRIT

Afghan-stitch crochet works great for kids' items, too! In this chapter are more ways to show off your mastery of this stitch and make super gifts for those precious folks who capture your pride and bring joy to your crafting.

For those kids who are fascinated with flags, space capsules, and Uncle Sam, the handmade projects on this page are a salute to their American spirit.

The star-spangled sweater, *opposite*, shows off our country's colors and makes a great warm-up for a small fry—in sizes 2, 4, and 6—for spring or fall outings.

Worked in the basic afghan stitch, the bodice is crocheted with two colors at the same time. Star appliqués set off the flag-blue yoke.

For smaller tots, make the blocks or bib *below*, using the same technique. Purchased appliqués of all kinds can decorate the plain sides of the blocks.

Instructions for all the terrific projects in this chapter begin on page 48.

This cheerful 33x44-inch afghan, *above,* dramatizes the entire spectrum of primary colors, and its childlike images speak for themselves.

Twenty blocks, worked in the basic afghan stitch, are decorated with favorite toddler cross-stitch motifs, such as bears, ducks, hearts, and boats. When all the blocks are assembled, two rounds of easy crocheting complete its scalloped border.

Infants will ride warm and comfortable in the pants, jacket, and cap *opposite.* Fashioned for 9- to 12-month-olds, this snowsuit sports an appealing texture and is decorated with colorful embroidered ribbings that keep out the cold.

All spruced up for a dressy spring outing, this young miss, *opposite,* sports a holiday coat of simple construction but interesting textural patterns.

The little girls' coat is designed for sizes 2, 4, and 6. The assembly of the coat pieces makes it easy to alter the lengths of both sleeves and skirt.

The afghan-knit stitch forms the bodice yoke on both the front and back. A detail of the coat back is *above*. A lacy shell stitch forms the sleeves and skirt.

Once you've mastered the techniques of these two versatile stitches, you'll discover countless other ways to create your own afghan-stitch projects. For example, the lacy stitch can easily be adapted to make a baby afghan, a shawl, or even a bedspread, using Size 10 thread with a Size 5 hook.

Patiently waiting for Mom to get on *her* sweater, the little one *opposite* is dressed for a spring ride on her backyard swing or a walk to the pond to feed the ducks.

We developed her sweater using the design for the coat on page 45, but adapted it for infants, sizes 6, 12, and 18 months. The bonnet uses the same lacy shell pattern and has satin ribbons that tie under the chin.

If you want to crochet a great gift that's sure to please a favorite child—neighbor, niece, or grandchild—the cap and mitten set *above* fills the bill and works up quickly. The tiny rosebuds and leaves are worked in at the same time you stitch the main portions of these accessories. With ribbings around the edges, the cap crown and mitten palms are worked in the afghan-knit stitch. The instructions include directions for making small, medium, and large children's sizes.

Red, White, and Blue Sweater

Shown on page 40.

Directions are for child's Size 2. Changes for sizes 4 and 6 follow in parentheses. Finished chest size = 24 (26½, 28) inches.

MATERIALS

Bernat Berella Sportspun (50-gram ball): 2 (2, 2) balls *each* of scarlet No. 2833 and white No. 2842; 1 (2, 2) ball of navy No. 2865
Size 6 afghan crochet hook or size to obtain gauge cited below
Size D crochet hook
Ten 1¼-inch star appliqués

Abbreviations: See page 7.
Gauge: With afghan hook, 5 afghan sts = 1 inch.

INSTRUCTIONS

BACK: With red yarn and afghan hook, ch 60 (66, 70).

For Size 2

Row 1 (first half): Keeping all lps on hook and using white yarn, insert hook in top lp of second ch from hook, yo and draw up lp; draw up lp in each of next 2 chs; drop white to back of work; * draw up 4 lps with red; drop red to back of back; draw up 4 lps with white; drop white to back of work; rep from * across row—60 (66, 70) lps on hook.

For Size 4

Row 1 (first half): Keeping all lps on hook and using red yarn, insert hook in top lp of second ch from hook, yo and draw up lp; draw up lp in each of next 2 chs, drop red to back of work; * using white yarn draw up 4 lps, drop white to back of work; draw up 4 lps with red, drop red to back of work; rep from * across row ending with 3 red lps.

For Size 6

Row 1 (first half): Keeping all lps on hook and using red yarn;

insert hook in top lp of second ch from hook, yo and draw up lp; draw up lp in each of next 3 chs, drop red to back of work; * using white yarn draw up 4 lps, drop white to back of work; draw up 4 lps with red, drop red to back of work; rep from * across row ending with 5 red lps.

For all sizes

Row 1 (second half): Changing color of yarn when only 1 lp of color in use remains on the hook and *always* dropping the yarn to the back of the work, yo, draw through first lp on hook, * yo, draw through 2 lps on hook; rep from * across row until 1 lp rem on hook. *Note:* On Size 2 and this row only, draw off the last red lp with white yarn.

Row 2 (first half): Keeping all lps on hook and keeping to color sequence as already established, sk first upright bar; * insert hook in next bar, yo and draw up lp; rep from * across row.

Row 2 (second half): Rep second half of Row 1.

Note: The lp rem at the end of the second half of all rows *always* counts as the first st of the next row.

Cont to work in stripe pattern as established for 7½ (8½, 9½) inches or for desired length to underarm; at end of last row, fasten off red and white yarns.

ARMHOLE SHAPING: Join the blue yarn and work even in basic afghan stitch until total length measures 12½ (14, 15½) inches, ending with second half of row. Sc across row picking up vertical lps to end off piece; fasten off.

FRONT: Work as for Back until length from beginning measures 11 (12½, 14) inches, ending with second half of row.

RIGHT NECK AND SHOULDER SHAPING: *Next row:* Sk first bar, draw up lps in next 15 (18, 21) sts. Work second half of row. *Next row:* Work across row, drawing up lps until 2 sts rem; **insert hook in each of next 2 vertical bars, yo, draw up lp—dec made;**

work second half of row. Cont to dec 1 st at neck edge every other row until 9 (12, 15) stitches rem, ending with second half of row.
Last row: Sc across row picking up vertical lps to finish off shoulder; fasten off.

LEFT NECK AND SHOULDER SHAPING: From left side count 15 (18, 21) sts and join blue yarn in next st to right. Draw up 15 (18, 21) lps across row. Work second half of row. Continue to work as for Right Shoulder reversing all shaping; fasten off.

SLEEVES (make 2): With red yarn, ch 32 (38, 44).

For Size 2

Working in basic afghan st as already established in Back and Front, draw up 3 lps with red—4 red lps on hook; * draw up 4 lps with white, draw up 4 lps with red; rep from * across row.

For Size 4

Working in basic afghan st, join white yarn and draw up 2 lps—3 lps on hook; * draw up 4 lps with red, draw up 4 lps with white; rep from * across row ending with 3 white lps.

For Size 6

Working in basic afghan st, draw up 3 lps with red—4 lps on hook; join white yarn, * draw up 4 lps with white, draw up 4 lps with red; rep from * across row ending with 4 white lps.

For all sizes

Next 3 rows: Cont to work even in stripe pattern as established.

Next row: Keeping to stripe pattern, sk first bar, **draw up lp in sp bet first and second bars—inc made;** work across row in basic afghan st until 1 st rem; work inc in next sp; draw up lp in last st.

Cont to inc 1 st each end every 6 (8, 9) rows until there are 46 (56, 64) sts. Work even in basic afghan st until sleeve measures 8 (9, 10) inches from beg; fasten off.

FINISHING: Sew shoulder seams; sew side seams below the blue area. Sew sleeve seams; sew sleeves to body of sweater along blue edges. Hand-sew 5 star appliqués to both the front and back of sweater.

NECK RIBBING: *Rnd 1:* With Size D crochet hook and blue yarn, work sc in each st around neck, making sure there is an *even* number of sts; join with sl st to first sc.

Rnd 2: Sc in first st, * **insert hook from back to front of next st and work sc—backward sc made;** sc in next st; rep from * around ending with a backward sc in last st.

Rep Rnd 2 for ribbing for 1 inch; fasten off.

WAIST AND SLEEVE RIBBING: Working with red yarn, rep instruction for Neck Ribbing around waist and sleeve edges, except work ribbings for 1½ inches; fasten off. Weave in all yarn ends.

Red, White, and Blue Baby Blocks

Shown on page 41.

Each block is a 4-inch cube.

MATERIALS
For set of 3
Pingouin Fil d'Écosse No. 3 (50-gram ball): 2 balls *each* of red No. 11, white No. 01, and navy No. 15
Size 6 afghan crochet hook
12 purchased appliqués with patriotic themes
4-inch-deep sheet of upholstery foam cut into 4-inch cubes

Abbreviations: See page 7.
Gauge: 5 afghan sts = 1 inch; 9 rows = 1 inch.

INSTRUCTIONS
To make 3 blocks
SIDE (make 6 white and 6 blue): With afghan hook and either white or blue thread, ch 20.

Row 1 (first half): Keeping all lps on hook, insert hook in top lp of second ch from hook, yo, draw up lp; * insert hook in top lp of next ch, yo, draw up lp; rep from * across row—20 lps on hook.

Row 1 (second half): Yo, draw through first lp on hook, * yo, draw through 2 lps on hook; rep from * across row.

Rows 2–36 (first half): Keeping all lps on hook, sk first upright bar, * insert hook in next bar and draw up lp; rep from * across row—20 lps on hook.

Rows 2–36 (second half): Rep second half of Row 1.

Next row: Sc across row, working scs around each vertical bar; fasten off.

STRIPED SIDE (make 6 red-and-white striped squares): With red, ch 20.

Follow instructions, *above,* for working in basic afghan, except make the following changes:

Row 1 (first half): Draw up 3 lps with red—4 lps on hook, drop red to back of work, * draw up 4 lps with white, drop white to back of work, draw up 4 lps with red, drop red to back of work; rep from * across row.

Row 1 (second half): Work off sts, drawing off red lps with red and white lps with white. Change color when only 1 lp of previous color remains on hook. Keeping to stripe pat, work even for total of 36 rows.

Next row: Sc across row, inserting hook under vertical lps. Sc red lps with red and white lps with white; fasten off.

FINISHING: Referring to photo on page 41 for placement of sides and using afghan hook as a regular crochet hook, sc squares together with red thread to form a cube. Leave one side free for stuffing. Center an appliqué on each plain-colored side and stitch in place with sewing thread. Weave in all thread ends. Insert foam cube into block and crochet shut; fasten off.

Red, White, and Blue Baby Bib

Shown on page 41.

MATERIALS
Pingouin Fil d'Écosse No. 3 (50-gram ball): 1 ball *each* of red No. 11, white No. 01, and navy No. 15
Four 1-inch white star appliqués
Size 6 afghan crochet hook
1 Size 3 coat snap

Abbreviations: See page 7.
Gauge: 5 afghan sts = 1 inch; 9 rows = 1 inch.

INSTRUCTIONS
Using single strand of red Fil d'Écosse, ch 18.

Row 1 (first half): Keeping all lps on hook insert hook in top lp of second ch from hook, yo and draw up lp; draw up lp in next ch, drop red to back of work; * using white yarn draw up 4 lps, drop white to back of work; draw up 4 lps with red, drop red to back of work; rep from * across row; end by drawing up lp in each of the last 3 chs.

Row 1 (second half): Changing color of yarn when only 1 lp of color in use remains on the hook and *always* dropping the yarn to the back of the work, yo, draw through first lp on hook, * yo, draw through 2 lps on hook; rep from * across row until 1 lp rem on hook.

Row 2 (increase row): Keeping to stripe pat, **draw up 2 lps in sp bet first and second bars—2 inc made,** draw up lp in second bar and each bar until 1 bar rem; draw up 2 lps in next sp, draw up lp in last bar—22 lps on hook; work second half of row.

Row 3: Work even.
Row 4: Rep Row 2—26 lps.
Row 5: Work even.
Row 6: Keeping to stripe pat, inc 1 st at each end—28 lps.
Row 7: Work even.
Rep rows 6 and 7 four more times—36 lps on hook.

continued

Work even until bib measures 6 inches from beg; cut and fasten off threads. Attach blue thread and work even until bib measures 8 inches from beg.

NECK SHAPING: Draw up 15 lps; work second half of row.

Next row: Draw up 13 lps, **insert hook under next 2 bars, yo, draw yarn through both bars—dec made**—14 lps on hook; work second half of row. Dec 1 st at neck edge every other row 3 times—11 lps. Work even until bib is 11¾ inches from beg.

SHOULDER SHAPING: Dec 1 st at shoulder edge every other row 3 times. Dec 2 sts at shoulder edge 1 time.

Work 1 row even; fasten off.

LEFT SIDE: Join blue thread 15 sts in from left edge. Draw up 15 lps. Work left side same as first, reversing all shaping. Weave in all threads.

TRIMMING THE BIB: With blue thread, sc in each st around upper half of bib; beg on right side where blue meets stripe, and end on left side where blue meets stripe; fasten off.

With red thread, sc in each st around bottom half of bib. Sew appliqué stars to bib. Sew coat snap to center back.

Baby Coverlet

Shown on page 42.

Afghan, including edging, measures 33x44 inches.

MATERIALS
Sport yarns in following amounts and colors: 10 ounces of bright yellow, 2 ounces *each* of red, orange, lime green, kelly green, turquoise, royal blue, purple, and magenta
Size F afghan crochet hook or size to reach following gauge
Size F crochet hook
Yarn needle

Abbreviations: See page 7.
Gauge: Over afghan stitch 5 sts = 1 inch.

INSTRUCTIONS
Note: The coverlet as shown on photo on page 42 has 3 blocks *each* crocheted with royal blue, magenta, and purple yarns and 2 squares *each* of all the remaining yarn colors except yellow. Yellow is used for the edging around the squares and coverlet border.

AFGHAN SQUARE (make 20): With any color, ch 26.
Row 1 (first half): Keeping all lps on hook, insert hook in top lp of second ch from hook, yo, draw up lp; * insert hook in top lp of next ch, yo, draw up lp; rep from * across row—26 lps on hook.
Row 1 (second half): Yo, draw through first lp on hook, * yo, draw through 2 lps on hook; rep from * across row.
Rows 2–26 (first half): Keeping all lps on hook, sk first upright bar, * insert hook in next bar and draw up lp; rep from * across row—26 lps on hook.
Rows 2–26 (second half): Rep second half of Row 1.
Row 27: Sk first bar, * **draw up lp in next bar and draw yarn through lp on hook—sl st made and 1 lp on hook;** rep from * across; fasten off.

CROSS-STITCHED BLOCKS: Using contrasting yarn colors for cross-stitches, center and embroider 10 blocks with the heart motif, *opposite, bottom left.* Embroider the remaining 10 blocks, working one of the motifs in each of the blocks. Refer to photo on page 42 for yarn color ideas.

BLOCK EDGING: *Rnd 1:* With right side of block facing and regular crochet hook, join yellow in any corner, ch 1, 3 sc in same sp, sc in each st around, working 3 sc in each corner; join with sl st in beg sc; fasten off.
Rnd 2: With right sides facing, join any one of yarn colors used for embroidery in any corner, ch 2, 2 hdc in same st; hdc in each st around, working 3 hdc in each corner; join to top of beg ch-2; fasten off.

Rnd 3: With right side facing, join yellow yarn in any corner, ch 3, 2 dc in same st as joining, dc in each st around, working 3 dc in each corner. Join with sl st in top of beg ch-3.

Join 4 squares for each of 5 rows as follows: With right sides together, sl st through corresponding back lps of each square, making sure designs are in same direction. Join rows in same way.

BORDER: *Rnd 1:* Join yellow in any corner, ch 1, 3 sc in same corner st; work sc evenly spaced around entire afghan, working 3 sc in each corner; join with sl st to beg sc.
Rnd 2: Sl st in next st, ch 4, 6 trc in same st; * sk 2 sts, sc in next st, sk 2 sts, 7 trc in next st; rep from * around, adjusting spacing to have 7 trc in each corner; join to beg ch; fasten off.

Infant Snowsuit

Shown on page 43.

Snowsuit fits infant 9–12 months old.

MATERIALS
Patons Astra acrylic sport yarn (50-gram ball): 8 balls of white (No. 2751); 1 ball of red (No. 2762)
Sizes G and J afghan crochet hooks
Size F crochet hook
Tapestry needle
6 small heart buttons

Abbreviations: See page 7.
Gauge: Using J hook, 5 pat cross-sts = 1 inch; using G hook, 5 stockinette stitches = 1 inch.

INSTRUCTIONS
For the snow pants
FIRST LEG: Beg with first leg at cuff, using white yarn, and Size G hook, ch 36.

continued

BABY COVERLET

1 Square = 1 Cross-Stitch

Row 1 (first half): Keeping all lps on hook, draw up lp in second ch from hook and in each ch across—36 lps on hook.

Row 1 (second half): Yo, draw through first lp on hook, * yo, draw through 2 lps on hook; rep from * across row.

Row 2 (first half): Keeping all lps on hook, * **insert hook from front to back bet the next vertical lp (bet front and back upright bars), draw up lp—k st made;** rep from * across row.

Row 2 (second half): Rep second half of Row 1.

Rows 3–10: Rep first and second halves of Row 2.

Row 11: Change to J afghan hook and work first half of increase row as follows: * (yo, pull up next lp as to k) 4 times, pull up next lp as to k; rep from * across—64 lps. Rep second half of Row 1.

Row 12 (first half): Ch 1, keeping all lps on hook, sk first bar; * sk next bar, draw up lp in next bar *knitwise;* draw up lp in skipped bar *knitwise;* rep from * across row.

Row 12 (second half): Rep second half of Row 1.

Rows 13–29: Rep Row 12; end with second half of row; fasten off and set first leg aside.

Make second leg; do not fasten off.

Note: Next row begins to work in rounds and joins the first leg to the second leg.

Rnd 30: Work across second leg in pat to last st, use this stitch along with the first st of the first leg to form a new cross-st pat, continue across first leg to end—63 cross-sts. Work second half of row over all sts. Place a pin at center of 32 cross-st pat to mark center front.

CROTCH SHAPING: Work across row to within 2 bars of pin; **insert hook under next 2 bars, yo, draw yarn through both bars—dec made;** work dec over next 2 bars; work even in pat across; work second half of row.

Work a dec *each* side of center pin on next 5 rows.

Work even in pat until piece measures 16½ inches above cuff.

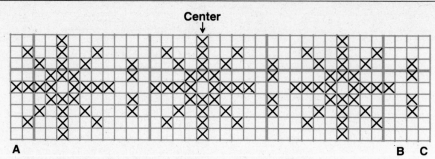

Center

DUPLICATE STITCH CHART FOR HAT AND LEG CUFF

A   B   C

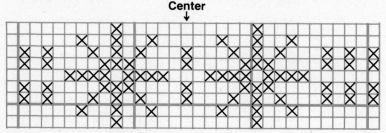

Center

DUPLICATE STITCH CHART FOR JACKET CUFF

WAISTBAND: Change to G hook and working in k st, dec as follows: (draw up 4 lps, work dec) 2 times; (draw up 1 lp, work dec) 30 times; (draw up 4 lps, work dec) 2 times; draw up last 4 lps—80 lps on hook; work second half of row.

Work even on 80 lps in k st for 9 rows; fasten off.

BIB: Sk next 27 sts. Attach yarn in next st and continue in k st on next 25 sts for bib. Work even until bib is 2¼ inches above waistband.

Buttonhole row (first half): Sk first upright bar, draw up 3 lps, sk next bar, draw up lp in each bar until 4 bars rem; sk next bar; draw up lp in last 3 bars. Work second half of row as follows: Work off 3 lps, ch 1, work off lps to 3 lps rem, ch 1, complete row.

Next row: Work next row in k st, drawing up lp in each bar and in each ch-1; work second half of row.

Work 2 more rows in k st; fasten off.

Sew center back and leg seams.

BACK BIB: Rep Bib directions, *above,* on center 25 sts of back until bib measures 3 inches above waistband; do not fasten off. Do not work buttonhole row.

Cont in k st on first 6 sts for strap; work even over these sts for

6 inches; fasten off. Attach yarn in sixth st from left side of back bib and work same number of rows as on first strap; fasten off.

With G hook work 1 row of reverse sc (crochet from left to right) loosely around each leg cuff. Beg at top of right strap work 1 row of reverse sc around entire upper edge of coveralls; fasten off. Weave in all ends. Steam lightly. Referring to duplicate st chart on page 31, embroider bib following chart, *opposite.* Embroider between A-C for leg cuffs following chart *above.*

For the cap

EARFLAP (make 2): With G hook, ch 10.

Row 1: Rep Row 1 of Snowsuit—10 lps on hook; work second half of row.

Row 2: Working in k st, draw up 2 lps, yo, draw up lps in each bar across row to within last 2 bars, yo, draw up 2 lps—12 lps on hook; rep second half of row.

Rep Row 2 until there are 20 lps on hook. Work even over 20 lps for 5 more rows; fasten off.

Make second flap.

HAT BODY: Attach yarn to last st on left side of either earflap, ch 30 for front of hat, join yarn to right side of second earflap; fasten off.

Join yarn to last st on left side of same earflap, ch 20; fasten off.

Attach yarn at beg of first earflap and draw up lps in each k st across; draw up lps in each of 30 chs, draw up lps across second earflap, and draw up lps in each of 20 chs; cont in k st for 9 more rows.

Change to Size J hook and work 10 rows of cross-st pat.

CROWN: *Row 1:* * Draw up 8 sts; work dec; rep from * across; complete second half of row.

Rep Row 1 until 9 sts rem; fasten off and pull end through rem 9 lps. Sew center seam.

With Size F hook, work 1 rnd reverse sc around edge of hat. Make one 2-inch pom-pom for top and two 1-inch pom-poms for earflaps. Sew pom-poms in place.

Work duplicate stitches on center hat front between A-B following chart, *opposite.*

For the jacket
BODICE: With J hook, ch 130

and rep Row 1 of Snowsuit. Work in cross-st pat until piece measures 7¼ inches or desired length to underarm; fasten off.

Place a pin between the 17th and 18th cross-sts from each end to divide fronts and back—30 cross-sts across back.

UPPER BODICE BACK AND SLEEVE BACKS (make 2): Ch 27; rep Row 1 of Snowsuit; fasten off and set aside. Make second piece; do not fasten off.

Row 2: Work across 27 lps in cross-st pat; continue across 30 cross-sts on back and across first piece with 27 lps—84 cross-sts.

Continue in cross-st pat until sleeve measures 4½ inches from beg ch; fasten off.

RIGHT FRONT: Beg at center front, work in cross-st pat across front to underarm, continue across right sleeve working into bottom of beg ch at underarm.

Work in pat until sleeve measures 3 inches from underarm.

NECK SHAPING: Sl st across 4 cross-sts; (work dec) twice; complete row in cross-st.

Rows 12–14: (Work dec) twice at neck edge and finish row in cross-st.

Rows 15 and 16: Work even in cross-st pat; fasten off.

CUFF: With Size G hook, draw up 32 lps along sleeve cuff edge. Work k st for 11 rows; fasten off.

LEFT FRONT: Rep Right Front, reversing all shapings.

FINISHING: Sew shoulder seams. With F hook, work 1 row reverse sc around cuff.

Draw up 64 lps around neck with G hook, work 3 rows k sts; fasten off.

Draw up 52 lps along each front with G hook, work 2 rows k sts; fasten off.

Work duplicate stitches on cuffs following jacket cuff chart, *opposite.* Overlap fronts 1½ inches. Sew two buttons just under neck border and 1½ inches apart. Sew remaining two buttons 2½ inches below the first two.

Child's Coat

Shown on pages 44–45.

Directions are for child Size 2; changes for sizes 4 and 6 are in parentheses. Finished chest = 24 (26, 28) inches.

MATERIALS
Patons Astra acrylic (50-gram ball): 5 (6, 7) balls of aqua (No. 2755); 1 ball *each* of white (No. 2751) and green (No. 2746)
Size 10 afghan crochet hooks, (standard and flexible) or size to reach gauge cited below
Size F crochet hook
Yarn needle
3 buttons, ⅝-inch diameter

Abbreviations: See page 7.
Gauge: With Size 10 hook, 10 sts and 9 rows of afghan crochet knit sts = 2 inches.

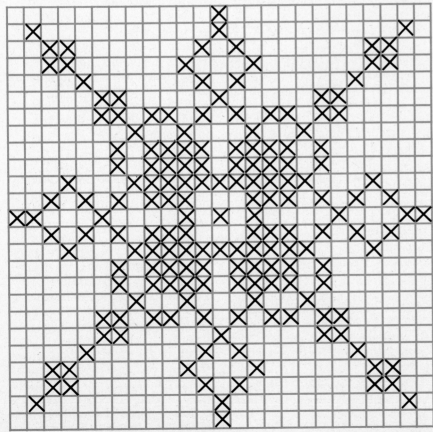

DUPLICATE STITCH CHART FOR BIB   **1 Block = 1 Stitch**

continued

INSTRUCTIONS

FRONT (side one): With Size 10 afghan hook and aqua yarn, ch 33 (35, 37).

Row 1 (first half): Keeping all lps on hook, draw up lp in second ch from hook and in each ch across row—33 (35, 37) lps on hook.

Row 1 (second half): Yo, draw through first lp on hook; * yo, draw through 2 lps on hook; rep from * across row.

Row 2 (first half): Keeping all lps on hook, sk first bar, * **insert hook from front to back bet the next vertical lp (bet front and back upright bars), draw up lp— k st made;** rep from * across row—33 (35, 37) lps on hook.

Row 2 (second half): Rep second half of Row 1.

Row 3 (3–4, 3–4): Rep Row 2.

Row 4 (5, 5): Keeping all lps on hook, sk first bar, draw up lp in next bar; **(insert hook through center of next 2 vertical lps, yo, draw through 2 lps—dec made) 2 times;** k 27 (29, 31)—31, (33, 35) lps on hook. Work second half of row until 28 (30, 32) lps are worked off hook, ch 2, work off rem 3 lps.

Row 5 (6, 6): Sk first bar, k 2, draw up lp in *each* of next 2 chs, k 28, (30, 32); work second half of row—33 (35, 37) lps on hook.

Rows 6–9 (7–10, 7–11): Rep Row 2.

Rows 10 and 11 (11–12, 12–13): Rep rows 4 and 5 (5 and 6, 5 and 6).

Row 12 (13, 14): Sk first bar, k 13 (14, 15), drop green to back of work; sk next 3 sts, with white, yo, insert hook *knitwise* in third st below the last skipped st and draw up lp; (yo, insert hook in same st and draw up lp) 9 times; yo, draw through 4 lps, (yo, draw through 5 lps) 3 times; drop white to back of work; with aqua, yo, draw through 5 lps, with aqua, working from right to left, (insert hook through center of 4-lp grp, and draw up lp) 4 times; sk 2 sts, k 14 (15, 16). Work second half of row.

Rows 13–15 (14–16, 15–17): Rep Row 2.

Rows 16 and 17 (17–18, 19–20): Rep rows 4–5 (5–6, 5–6).

Rows 18 and 19 (19–21, 21–23): Rep Row 2; fasten off.

NECK SHAPING: *Row 20 (22, 24):* Sk 13 (14, 15) sts; join aqua in next st, k 1, work dec, k 16 (17, 18); work second half of row.

Row 21 (23, 25): Sk first st, k 18 (19, 20).

Row 22 (24, 26): Sk first st, k 1, work dec, k 15 (16, 17).

Row 23 (25, 27): Sk first st, k 17 (18, 19).

Row 24 (26, 28): Sk first st, k 1, work dec, k 14 (15, 16).

Rows 25–27 (27–31, 29–35): Sk first st, k 17 (18, 19); fasten off.

FRONT (side two): Work as for side one through Row 3 (4, 4).

Rows 4–11 (5–12, 5–13): Sk first st, k 32 (34, 36).

Row 12 (13, 14): Rep Row 12 (13, 14) of side one.

Rows 13–19 (14–21, 15–23): Sk first st, k 32, (34, 36).

NECK SHAPING: *Row 20 (22, 24):* Sk first st, k 15 (16, 17), work dec, k 2.

Row 21 (23, 25): Sk first st, k all sts.

Row 22 (24, 26): Sk first st, k 14 (15, 16), work dec, k 2.

Row 23 (25, 27): Sk first st, k all sts across row.

Row 24 (26, 28): Sk first st, k 13 (14, 15), work dec, k 2.

Rows 25–27 (27–31, 29–35): Sk first st, k 16 (17, 18); fasten off.

BACK: With Size 10 afghan hook and aqua yarn, ch 61 (65, 69).

Row 1: Rep Row 1 of Front—61 (65, 69) lps on hook.

Row 2: Sk first st, k 60 (64, 68) sts across row.

Rows 3–24 (3–28, 3–32): Rep Row 2.

RIGHT NECK SHAPING: *Row 25 (29, 33):* Sk first st, k 14 (15, 16), work dec, k 2.

Row 26 (30, 34): Sk first st, k all sts across row.

Row 27 (39, 35): Sk first st, k 13 (14, 15), work dec, k 2; fasten off.

LEFT NECK SHAPING: *Row 25 (29, 33):* Sk next 23 (25, 27) sts; join yarn and k 1 in next st, k 1, work dec, k 15 (16, 17).

Row 26 (30, 34): Sk first st, k all sts across row.

Row 27 (31, 35): Sk first st, k 1, work dec, k 14 (15, 16); fasten off.

With right sides facing and Size F hook, sl st Front Sides to Back at shoulder seams.

SLEEVES: *Row 1 (first half):* With right side facing and afghan hook, work along shoulder edge as follows: Sk first 3 sts, * insert hook under both lps of next st and draw up lp; rep from * across edge until there are 48 (56, 64) lps on hook.

Row 1 (second half): Yo, draw through 2 lps on hook, * ch 4, **yo, draw through 5 lps on hook— shell made;** rep from * across until 3 lps rem on hook; ch 3, yo, draw through 3 lps, ch 1.

Note: In next row, draw up lps only in top lps of chs; do not draw up lps in top of shells.

Row 2 (first half): Draw up lp in third ch of ch-3; * insert hook under next ch and draw up lp; rep from * across row.

Row 2 (second half): Rep second half of Row 1.

Rows 3–21 (3–26, 3–31): Rep Row 2; fasten off.

Work second sleeve along opposite shoulder edge.

With right sides facing and F hook, sl st sleeve underarms and side seams tog.

SKIRT: *Row 1 (first half):* With right side facing, and flexible afghan hook, work along the lower edge of bodice (holding work upside down) as follows: Insert hook through center of next vertical lp, yo, draw up lp; (insert hook through center of next vertical lp, yo, draw up lp) 5 times; * insert hook through center of next vertical lp, yo, draw up lp, insert hook *between* next 2 vertical lps, yo, draw up lp; rep from * across row until 5 lps rem; (insert hook through center of next vertical lp, yo, draw up lp) 5 times—244 (260, 276) lps on hook.

Row 1 (second half): Rep second half of Row 1 of Sleeve.

Rows 2–33 (2–38, 2–43): Rep Row 2 of Sleeve; fasten off.

FINISHING: With right side facing and F crochet hook, work 1 rnd of sc around hem and inner front and neckline edges, working 2 sc in *each* corner; join with sl st to first sc; do not turn. Work 1 rnd reverse sc (work from left to right); join to first sc; fasten off.

Work around each sleeve cuff in same manner.

With tapestry needle and double strand of green yarn, embroider 3 lazy daisy sts at base of each white motif. Sew on buttons.

Pink Sweater and Bonnet Set

Shown on page 46.

Directions are for infant Size 6 months. Changes for sizes 12 and 18 months are in parentheses. Finished chest = 16 (18, 20) inches.

MATERIALS
Patons Valencia (50-gram ball):
2 (3, 4) balls pink (MC) No. 2424; 1 ball *each* of white (CC) No. 2422 white and salmon (A) No. 2431
Size 10 afghan crochet hook or size to obtain gauge cited below; Size F crochet hook
Yarn needle
Three buttons, ⅜ inch in diameter
½ yard ⅜-inch-wide pink ribbon

Abbreviations: See page 7.
Gauge: With Size 10 afghan hook, 21 sts and 19 rows of afghan knit sts = 4 inches.

INSTRUCTIONS
For the sweater
FRONT: *Side One:* With Size 10 hook and MC, ch 20 (22, 24).
Foundation row (first half): Keeping all lps on hook, draw up lp in second ch from hook and in each ch—20 (22, 24) lps on hook.
Foundation row (second half): Yo, draw through first lp on hook; * yo, draw through 2 lps on hook; rep from * across until 1 lp on hook. *Rep for all second halves of rows throughout.*

Row 1: Keeping all lps on hook, sk first st, * **insert hook from front to back bet the next vertical lp (bet front and back upright bars), draw up lp—k st made;** rep from * across row.
Rows 2–5 (6, 7): Rep Row 1.
Row 6, (7, 8): Sk first st, k 6 (7, 8), drop MC to back of work, sk next 3 sts, with CC, yo, insert hook *knitwise* in third st below the last skipped st and draw up lp, (yo, insert hook into same st, yo, draw up a lp) 9 times, yo, draw through 4 lps on hook, (yo, draw through 5 lps) 3 times, drop CC to back of work; with MC, yo, draw through 5 lps. With MC, (insert hook through center of 4-lp grp, yo, draw up a lp) 4 times, sk 2 sts, k 8 (9, 10).
Rows 7–10 (8–11, 9–12): Sk first st, k 19 (21, 23). Fasten off.
Row 11 (12, 13): Sk first 6 (7, 8) sts, rejoin yarn by knitting into 7th (8th, 9th) st, k 1, k 2 tog, k 10 (11, 12).
Row 12 (13, 14): Sk first st, k 12 (13, 14).
Row 13 (14, 15): Sk first st, k 2 tog, k 9 (10, 11).
Rows 14–18 (15–20, 16–22): Sk first st, k 11 (12, 13); fasten off.

SIDE TWO: Work as for Side One through Row 5 (6, 7).
Row 6 (7, 8): Sk first st, k 7 (8, 9), drop MC to back of work, sk next 3 sts, with CC, yo, insert hook *knitwise* in third st below the last skipped st and draw up lp, (yo, insert hook into same st, yo, draw up a lp) 9 times, yo, draw through 4 lps on hook, (yo, draw through 5 lps) 3 times, drop CC to back of work; with MC, yo, draw through 5 lps. With MC, (insert hook through center of 4 lp group, yo, draw up a lp) 4 times, sk 2 sts, k 7 (8, 9).
Rows 7–10 (8–11, 9–12): Work as for Side One.
Row 11, (12, 13): Sk first st, k 9 (10, 11), k 2 tog, k 2.
Row 12 (13, 14): Sk first st, k 12 (13, 14).
Row 13 (14, 15): Sk first st, k 8 (9, 10), k 2 tog, k 2.
Rows 14–18 (15–20, 16–22): Work as for Side One; fasten off.

BACK: With Size 10 hook and MC, ch 41 (45, 49). Work foundation row.
Row 1: Sk first st, k 40 (44, 48).
Rows 2–15 (17, 19): Rep Row 1.

NECK SHAPING: *Row 16 (18, 20):* Sk first st, k 9 (10, 11), k 2 tog, k 2.
Row 17 (19, 21): Sk first st, k 12 (13, 14).
Row 18 (20, 22): Sk first st, k 8 (9, 10), k 2 tog, k 2; fasten off.
Beg to work opposite side of neck: Sk 13 (15, 17) sts, rejoin yarn by knitting into 14th (16th, 18th) st, k 1, k 2 tog, k 10 (11, 12).
Row 17, (19, 21): Sk first st, k 12 (13, 14).
Row 18 (20, 22): Sk first st, k 1, k 2 tog, k 9 (10, 11); fasten off.
Using F crochet hook and MC, and with right sides facing, sl st fronts to back at shoulder seams.

SLEEVES: *Row 1* (first half): With right side facing, MC and afghan hook, work along shoulder edge, sk foundation row, * insert hook under both lps of next st, yo, draw up lp; rep from * until there are 36 (40, 44) lps on hook.
Row 1 (second half): Yo, draw through 2 lps, * ch 4, yo, draw through 5 lps; rep from * across until 3 lps rem on hook, ch 3, yo, draw through 3 lps, ch 1.
Row 2 (first half): Insert hook under top lp of third ch of ch-3, yo, draw lp through ch, * insert hook under top lp only of next ch, yo, draw a lp through ch; rep from * across. *Note:* Only the chains of previous rows are worked; tops of shells are skipped.
Row 2 (second half): Rep second half of Row 1.
Rows 3–15 (17, 19): Rep Row 2; fasten off. Rep Sleeve instructions on opposite side.
Using F crochet hook and MC, and with right sides facing, sl st underarm sleeve seams.

SKIRT: *Row 1* (first half): With right side facing, MC and flexible afghan hook, work along the lower edge of bodice, (holding work)
continued

upside down) as follows: * **Insert hook from front to back bet the first vertical lp (bet front and back upright bars), yo, draw up lp—k st made;** * k 2, insert hook bet vertical lps (under ch), yo, draw up a lp; rep from * across; end k 2—120 (132, 144) lps on hook.

Row 1 (second half): Rep second half of Row 1 of Sleeve.

Row 2: Rep Row 2 of Sleeve.

Rows 3–14 (16, 18): Rep Row 2; fasten off.

FINISHING: With right side facing and Size F hook, sc around all edges working 2 sc in lower and upper front corners; join with sl st to first sc; do not turn. Work 1 row reverse sc (work from left to right); join to first sc; fasten off. Work around cuffs in same manner. Using tapestry needle and double strand of Color A, embroider three lazy daisy sts at base of each crown stitch.

Mark placements for 3 button lps. With right side facing, work into back of sc edging row as follows: Sl st in st before lp placement, sl st in next st, ch 5, sl st in same st, sl st in next st; fasten off. Rep for each button lp. Sew buttons opposite lps.

For the bonnet
BACK: With MC and afghan hook, ch 17 (19, 21). Work foundation row as for sweater.

Row 1: Sk first st, k 16 (18, 20).

Rows 2–7 (8, 9): Rep Row 1.

Row 8 (9, 10): K 6 (7, 8), drop MC to back of work, sk next 3 sts, with CC, yo, insert hook *knitwise* in third st below the last skipped st and draw up lp, (yo, insert hook into same st, yo, draw up a lp) 9 times, yo, draw through 4 lps on hook, (yo, draw through 5 lps) 3 times, drop CC to back of work; with MC, yo, draw through 5 lps. With MC, (insert hook through center of 4-lp grp, yo, draw up a lp) 4 times, sk 2 sts, k 6 (7, 8).

Rows 9–15 (10–17, 11–19): Sk first st, k 16 (18, 20).

Row 16 (18, 20): Sk first st, k 1, **insert hook bet lps under ch, yo, draw up a lp—inc made;** (k 1, inc 1) 2 (3, 4) times, k 4, inc 1, k 5, inc 1, (k 1, inc 1) 2 (3, 4) times, k 2—24 (28, 32) sts.

Row 17 (19, 21) (first half): Sk first st, k across.

Row 17 (19, 21) (second half): Yo, draw through 2 lps, * ch 4, yo, draw through 5 lps, rep from * across until 3 lps on hook; ch 3, yo, draw through 3 lps, ch 1.

Row 18 (20, 22): Insert hook under top lp of third ch of ch-3, yo draw up lp; * insert hook under top lp of next ch, yo, draw up lp; rep from * across. Rep second half of Row 17 (19, 21).

Rows 19–25 (21–28, 23–31): Rep Row 18 (20, 22); fasten off.

SIDE ONE: *Row 1* (first half): With right side facing, MC, and afghan hook, and working along one side edge, insert hook under both lps of starting ch, yo, draw up lp; * insert hook under both lps of next st, yo, draw up a lp; rep from * 11 more times; (in next st, insert hook under top lp only, yo, draw up lp, insert hook under both lps of same st, yo, draw up lp) 3 (5, 7) times, insert hook under both lps of next st, yo, draw up lp—20 (24, 28) lps on hook. Rep second half of Row 17 (19, 21) of Bonnet Back.

Row 2: Rep Row 18 (20, 22) of Bonnet Back.

Rows 3–9 (10, 11): Rep Row 2; fasten off.

SIDE TWO: *Row 1* (first half): With right side facing, MC and afghan hook, work along opposite edge, insert hook under both lps of Row 16 (18, 20) of Bonnet Back; (insert hook under top lp of next st, yo, draw up lp, insert hook under both lps of same st, yo, draw up lp) 3 (5, 7) times; * insert hook under both lps of next st, yo, draw up lp; rep from * 11 more times; insert hook under both lps of starting ch, yo, draw up lp—20 (24, 28) lps. Rep second half of Row 1 of Side One.

Rows 2–9 (10, 11): Work as for Side One; fasten off.

With right sides facing, sl st bonnet sides to bonnet back.

FINISHING: With right side facing, sc along bottom edge of bonnet, ch 3, turn.

Next row: Dc in same st, ch 1; * sk sc, dc in each of next 2 dc, ch 1; rep from * 3 (4, 5) more times, sk 1 st, 2 dc in next st, ch 1; rep bet * 6 times, sk 1 st, 2 dc in next st, ch 1, rep bet *s 4 (5, 6) times; sk 1 st, 2 dc in next st, ch 1, turn.

Next row: Sc around entire bonnet, working 2 sc in each corner; join to first sc; do not turn.

Last row: Work 1 row of reverse sc around; fasten off. Embroider 3 lazy daisy sts at base of crown stitch in same manner as for sweater. Secure and trim loose ends. Weave ribbon through ribbon openings.

Rosebud Hat and Mitten Set

Shown on page 47.

Directions are for child's Size Small (3–5). Changes for Medium (6–8) are in parentheses. Mittens fit hand measurement of 4–4½ (5–5½) inches. Hat fits crown measurement of 19 (20) inches.

MATERIALS
Patons Astra sport yarns (50-gram ball): 3 balls of white (No. 2751); 1 ball *each* of aqua (No. 2755) and rose (No. 2786)
Sizes 8, 9, and 10.5 afghan crochet hooks or sizes to reach gauge cited below
Size G crochet hook
Stitch holder

Abbreviations: See page 7.
Gauge: With 10.5 hooks, 9 sts and 9 rows in afghan crochet knit sts = 2 inches.

INSTRUCTIONS
For the hat
With Size 8 afghan hook and white yarn, ch 103 (107).

Row 1 (first half): Keeping all lps on hook, insert hook in second ch from hook, yo, draw up lp; * insert hook in next ch, yo, draw up lp; rep from * across row—103 (107) lps on hook.

Row 1 (second half): Yo, draw through first lp on hook; * yo, draw through 2 lps on hook; rep from * across until 1 lp rem on hook.

RIBBING: *Row 1* (first half): Keeping all lps on hook, sk first st; **holding yarn at back of work, insert hook, from front to back, through center of next vertical lp, yo, draw up lp—k st made;** k 1; **holding yarn in front of work, insert hook, from back to front, through center of next vertical lp, yo, draw up lp—p st made;** * k 3, p 1; rep from * across row until 3 lps rem; k 3.

Row 1 (second half): Yo, draw through first lp on hook; * yo, draw through 2 lps on hook; rep from * across row until 1 lp rem on hook.

Rows 2–6: Rep Row 1. At end of Row 6, change to 10.5 hook.

CROWN: *Row 1:* Sk first bar; k all sts—103 (107) lps on hook.

Rows 2–4: Rep Row 1.

Row 5: Sk first bar, k 1 (3); * drop white to back of work, sk 2 sts; **with aqua, trc around st 3 rows below the next st, drop aqua to back of work; with white, k 1 into second st of the 2 skipped sts, drop white to back of work; with aqua, trc into same st as last trc, drop aqua to back of work; sk st behind last trc, with white, k 1 into next st, drop white to back of work; with aqua, trc into same st as last trc, drop aqua to back of work—leaf, stem pat made;** sk st, with white, k 3; rep from * across until 6 (8) sts rem; work leaf, stem pat over next 5 sts; k 1 (3)—103 (107) lps.

Row 6: Sk first bar, k all sts.

Row 7: Sk first bar, k 3 (5); * drop white to back of work; **with rose, yo, insert hook knitwise into next st, yo, draw up lp, (yo, insert hook into same st, yo, draw up a lp) 4 times; drop rose to back of work; with white, yo, draw through 10 lps, yo, draw through 1 lp—bobble made;** k 7; rep from * across until 4 (6) lps rem; work bobble in next st; with white, k 3 (5).

Rows 8–19 (8–21): K all sts.

Row 20 (22): Sk first st, * k 2, **insert hook knitwise through center of next 2 vertical lps, yo, draw through 2 lps—dec made;** rep from * across until 3 lps rem; k 3.

Row 21 (23): K all sts.

Row 22 (24): Sk first st, * k 1, work dec; rep from * across until 3 lps rem; k 3.

Row 23 (25): K all sts.

Row 24 (26): Sk first st, k 1, * work dec; rep from * across until 2 lps rem; k 2.

Row 25 (27): K all sts.

Row 26 (28): Rep Row 24 (26); end k 1 (2).

Row 27 (29) (first half): K all sts.

Row 27 (29) (second half): Yo, draw through all 15 (16) lps on hook; fasten off. Sl st back edges of hat together; fasten off.

Sc around bottom edge of hat; join with sl st to first sc; do not turn. Work 1 rnd of reverse sc (crochet from left to right); join to first sc; fasten off.

For the mittens

RIGHT MITTEN: With Size 9 afghan hook and white yarn, ch 27 (31). *Row 1:* Rep Row 1 of hat.

Rows 2–11: Rep Row 1 of hat Ribbing; at end of Row 11, change to 10.5 hook.

HAND: *Rows 1–7 (8):* K all sts.

THUMB OPENING: *Row 8 (9):* Sk first bar, k 15 (17); work off sts as for basic afghan st; sl yarn end st to holder; sk 3 sts, join separate strand of yarn in next st; k 8 (10), work off sts as for basic afghan st, ch 3; fasten off.

Row 9 (10): Sl yarn end st off holder and put back on hook, k 16 (18), draw up lps in each of the 3 chs, k 8 (10).

Rows 10–13 (11–14): K all sts.

Row 14 (15): Sk first bar, k 4 (5), with aqua work leaf, stem pat over next 5 sts; with white k 17 (20). Work off all lps with white on second half of row.

Row 15 (16): K all sts.

Row 16 (17): Sk first bar, k 6 (7), work bobble in next st with rose; with white k 19 (22).

Rows 17–22 (18–24): K all sts.

Row 23 (25): K 2, * work dec, k 6 (8), work dec *; k 3, rep bet *s; k 2. *Row 24 (27):* K 2, * work dec, k 4 (6), work dec *; k 3, rep bet *s; k 2.

Row 25 (28): K 2, * work dec, k 2 (4), work dec *; k 3, rep bet *s; k 2. *Row 26 (29):* K 2, * work dec, k 0 (2), work dec *; k 3, rep bet *s; k 2.

Row 27 (30) (first half): K all sts.

Row 27 (30) (second half): Yo, draw through all 11 (15) lps on hook; fasten off. Draw yarn end through last lp on hook and pull tightly to gather.

THUMB (first side): *Row 1:* Insert hook *knitwise* into st beside bottom right of thumb opening, yo, draw up lp, draw up lps in each of the 3 sts skipped in Row 8, draw up lp in st at left side of thumb opening—5 lps on hook. Work second half of row.

Rows 2–9 (11): K all sts.

Row 10 (12): K 1, work dec, k 2.

Row 11 (13): K 1, work dec, k 1; fasten off.

Turn work cuff side up and work into other side of opening same as for first side, through Row 9 (11).

Row 10 (12): K 2, work dec, k 1.

Row 11 (13): Rep Row 11 (13) of First Side.

Push thumb sides to wrong side of work and sl st sides tog.

With right sides facing, sl st mitten sides tog.

LEFT MITTEN: Work as for Right Mitten through Row 7 (8).

Row 8 (9): Sk first bar, k 7, (9), work off and sl yarn end st to holder; sk 3 sts, join separate strand of yarn in next st, k 16 (18); work second half of row; ch 3, fasten off.

Row 9 (10): Sl yarn end st off holder and place back on hook, k 8 (10), draw up lps in each of next 3 chs, k 16 (18).

Rows 10–13 (11–14): Work same as for Right Mitten.

Row 14 (15): Sk first bar, k 16 (19), with aqua work leaf, stem pat over next 5 sts; k 5 (6).

Row 15 (16): K all sts.

Row 16 (17): Sk first bar, k 18 (21), work bobble with rose; with white, k 7 (8).

Complete Left Mitten following instructions for Right Mitten.

AFGHANS AND THROWS

COUNTRY WARMTH, COUNTRY STYLE

♦ ♦ ♦

If you're one of those crocheters who spends all of her free time stitching one afghan after another, then glance through this chapter to find eight striking projects. You'll find afghans worked in blocks, in panels, and in one large piece—like the throw *opposite*. Here, too, are more afghan stitch variations that shape into lots of surprising textures.

The bright pink 38x50-inch afghan, *right,* romanticizes the hefty versions of Fisherman knitting. You'll use crocheting stitches to imitate knit and purl stitches, and post crochet stitches to pattern the graceful cables and treelike branches. The soft brushed yarn creates an airy lush throw that you'll want to use every season of the year.

Crocheted in one large piece with sport-weight yarn, this project requires a flexible afghan hook to hold all of the 189 stitches.

Because this afghan is a challenging project, you might want to practice working the four patterns with scrap yarns before you begin.

You also can crochet this afghan with worsted-weight yarns to create a larger throw that can easily be used as a twin-size bed cover.

Instructions for all the afghans and throws in this chapter begin on page 68.

On the chilly days of winter, you'll love covering yourself with the 48x60-inch floral afghan *above*.

This bed-of-tulips afghan is an arrangement of 36 white 7½x9½-inch blocks that are all worked in the basic afghan stitch. Then, tulips are cross-stitched atop each block, using warm peach, yellow, and rose yarn colors or yarn colors to match those of your favorite comfy hangout.

Outline each block with a round of peach single crochets. Then assemble the blocks with crochet stitches, as we did, or sew them together using whipstitches. A flowing scalloped border completes this afghan.

Let your imagination take over when you make the 46x64-inch afghan *above,* with its contrasting combinations of textures and colors. All blocks are 8½ inches square, and the nubby bobble blocks complement the flat, even weave of the other blocks, which resemble the stockinette stitches of knitting.

Use yarn in your scrap bag to make colorful bobble blocks, if you wish. But stitch each stockinette block with one yarn color because you'll embellish these blocks with a floral motif using duplicate stitch embroidery with the remains of your yarn scraps.

Designs from quilts translate beautifully into afghan stitch projects. The lap robes here, which use the patterns of Aunt Sukie's Choice, *left,* or Trip-Around-the-World, *opposite,* capture the warmth and charm of these two favorite coverlets.

Both of these lap throws use the same stitches and techniques for assembling the strips. Once you've made either one of these robes, you quickly can adapt this method to create any other crocheted quilt patterns that call for rectangles, squares, and triangles.

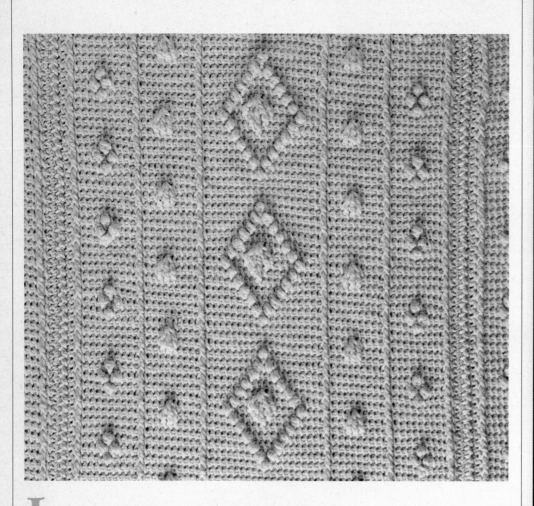

If you want to make a terrific gift for Dad for Father's Day or for a young man who's going off to college, the afghan *opposite* is most appropriate and sure to please.

This 52x62-inch afghan uses the basic afghan stitch to establish its background and is topped with an arrangement of raised popcorns and clusters to give the afghan its old-world character.

Use worsted-weight yarn to crochet each of the three panels. (The photo *above* shows the detail of the 65 stitches in each of the panels.)

You can either sew the panels together or join them using a combination of single crochets and chain stitches, as specified in the instructions. Then, add hefty knotted fringe to set off the afghan's mannish and sporty qualities.

It's fun to watch the crocheted afghan at *left* take shape row by row and reveal its diagonal star stitch design.

Worked with worsted-weight yarn, the afghan requires a flexible afghan hook to hold all of the 196 stitches.

Rounds of single and double crochets and a wavy shell-stitch pattern edge this 55x67-inch afghan to complete its 2-inch-wide border.

Like the icing on a cake, the colorful frosted squares of the afghan *above* will whet the appetite of eager crocheters. You'll want to use brushed acrylic yarns to create its airy loftiness. A wonderful scrap and take-along project, this 58x67-inch afghan works up quickly.

Pink Fisherman Throw

Shown on pages 58 and 59.

Throw measures 38x50 inches, less fringe.

MATERIALS
Brunswick Sportmist, 100% brushed acrylic (50-gram ball): 15 balls of hot pink (No. 8804)
Size 10 flexible afghan crochet hook
Size F crochet hook
Cable needle

Abbreviations: See page 7.
Gauge: 10 sts and 9 rows of afghan knit sts = 2 inches.

INSTRUCTIONS
Note: To work k st, **keeping yarn at back of work, insert hook from front to back bet the next vertical lp (bet front and back upright bars), draw up lp.**

To work p st, **bring yarn to front of work, insert hook from back through center of next vertical lp to the front of the work, yo, draw up lp.**

All second halves of rows, except the second half of Row 1 of Pattern 2, are worked as follows: Yo, draw through the first lp on the hook, * yo, draw through 2 lps on hook; rep from * until 1 lp rem on hook.

PATTERN 1 (worked over 39 sts): *Row 1* (first half): Keeping all lps on hook, sk first st, k 5; * **trc around the st 3 rows below the second st to the left—post-trc made;** k 4, trc around same st as previous trc, k 4; rep from * 2 more times; end trc around st 3 rows below the second st to the left, k 4, trc around same st as previous trc, k 5.
Rows 2 and 3 (first half): K all sts.
Rep rows 1–3 for Pattern 1.

PATTERN 2 (worked over 6 sts): *Row 1* (first half): P 1, k 4, p1.
Row 1 (second half): Draw off lps in the usual manner until the first p st in Pattern 2 is drawn off hook; drop first lp from hook. *Note:* Hereafter, when lp is dropped from hook, it will be called the "yarn-end-st." Sl next 2 lps to cable needle and hold in back of work, sl yarn-end-st back on hook, yo, draw through 2 lps on hook; drop yarn-end-st from hook, sl lps from cable needle back onto hook, sl yarn-end-st back onto hook, work off rem lps in the usual manner.
Rows 2–6 (first half): P 1, k 4, p 1. Rep rows 1–6 for Pattern 2.

PATTERN 3 (worked over 35 sts): Row 1 (first half): K 6, work post-trc, k 4, trc around same st as last trc, k 6; work post-trc; (k 2, trc around same st as last trc) 2 times; end k 6, work post-trc; k 4, trc around same st as last trc; k 5.
Rows 2 and 3 (first half): K all sts across row.
Row 4 (first half): K 6, work post-trc, k 4, trc around same st as previous trc; k 6, (trc around post-trc below, k 2) 2 times; trc around post-trc below; k 6, work post-trc, k 4, trc around same st; k 5.
Rows 5 and 6 (first half): K all sts across row.
Row 7 (first half): K 6, work post-trc, k 4, trc around same st as last trc, k 6, trc around center post-trc, (k 2, trc around center post-trc) 2 times; k 6, work post-trc, k 4, trc around same st as last trc, k 5.
Rep rows 2–7 for Pattern 3.

PATTERN 4 (worked over 29 sts): *Row 1* (first half): K 1, * work post-trc, k 4, trc around same st as previous trc; k 4; rep from * 2 more times; work post-trc, k 4, trc around same st as previous trc.
Rows 2 and 3 (first half): K all sts across the row.
Row 4 (first half): * K 1, trc around post-trc below, k 4, trc around post-trc directly below, k 3; rep from * 2 more times; k 1, trc around post-trc directly below, k 4, trc around post-trc below.
Rows 5 and 6 (first half): K all sts across the row.
Row 7 (first half): K 2, * yo hook twice, draw up lp around post-trc to right, (yo, draw through 2 lps on hook) 2 times; k 1; yo hook twice, draw up lp around post-trc to left, (yo, draw though 2 lps on hook) 2 times; yo, draw through 3 lps on hook; k 7; rep from * 2 more times; yo hook twice, draw up lp around post-trc to right, (yo, draw through 2 lps on hook) 2 times; k 1; yo hook twice, draw up lp around post-trc to left, (yo, draw though 2 lps on hook) 2 times; yo, draw through 3 lps on hook; k 2.
Rows 8 and 9 (first half): K all sts across the row.
Row 10 (first half): K 1, * trc around trc-grp below, k 4, trc around same trc-grp; k 4; rep from * 2 more times; trc around trc-grp below, k 4, trc around same trc-grp.
Rep rows 2–10 for Pattern 4.

AFGHAN: With flexible afghan hook, ch 189.
Row 1 (first half): Retaining all lps on hook, draw up lp in second ch from hook and in each ch across row—189 lps on hook.
Row 1 (second half): Yo, draw through first lp on hook, * yo, draw through 2 lps on hook; rep from * across row.
Row 2 (first half): Sk first st, k 38; p 1, k 4, p 1, k 99; p 1, k 4, p 1, k 39.
Row 2 (second half): Rep second half of Row 1.
Rows 3–5: Rep Row 2.
Rows 6–221: Beg with Row 1 for all patterns, work the 3 rows of Pat 1 over the first 39 sts; 6 rows of Pat 2 over the next 6 sts; 6 rows of Pat 3 over the next 35 sts; 10 rows of Pat 4 over next 29 sts; 6 rows of Pat 3 over next 35 sts; 6 rows of Pat 2 over the next 6 sts; and 3 rows of Pat 1 over rem 39 sts. There will be 24 repeats of Pat 4 when work is complete.

FINISHING: Using Size F crochet hook, work 1 row of sc along each long end of afghan. Work 2 rows of sc along each short end.
Cut 14-inch lengths of yarn for fringe. In bundles of 5 strands and with wrong side of afghan facing, work knot fringe evenly spaced across both short ends. Trim ends even.

Tulip Afghan

Shown on page 60.

Afghan measures 48x60 inches.

MATERIALS
Bernat Sportspun (50-gram
ball) in the following amounts
and colors: 15 balls of white
(No. 2842); 4 balls of peach
blossom (No. 2870); 2 balls of
peacock (No. 2881); 1 ball
each of canary (No. 2803) and
rose heather (No. 2837)
Size H afghan crochet hook
Size H crochet hook
Graph paper
Yarn tapestry needle

Abbreviations: See page 7.
Gauge: 1 block = 7½x9½ inches.

INSTRUCTIONS
    BLOCK (make 36): With afghan
hook and white, ch 40.
    Row 1 (first half): Keeping all
lps on hook, insert hook in top lp
of second ch from hook, yo, draw
up lp; * insert hook in top lp of
next ch, yo, draw up lp; rep from *
across row—40 lps on hook.
    Row 1 (second half): Yo, draw
through first lp on hook, * yo,
draw through 2 lps on hook; rep
from * across row.
    Rows 2–39 (first half): Keeping
all lps on hook, sk first upright
bar, * insert hook in next bar and
draw up lp; rep from * across
row—40 lps on hook.
    Rows 2–39 (second half): Rep
second half of Row 1.
    Row 40: Sk first bar, **draw up
lp in next bar and draw yarn
through lp on hook—sl st made
and 1 lp on hook;** rep from *
across; fasten off.

    STITCHED TULIP MOTIFS:
With tapestry needle and noting
center of the tulip motif chart,
above, cross-stitch a tulip in each
block. *Note:* The diagram for motif is on a 26x40-st grid. Make
sure the motif is centered on your
40x40-st block. Refer to page 7
for instructions for working
cross-stitches onto afghan stitch.

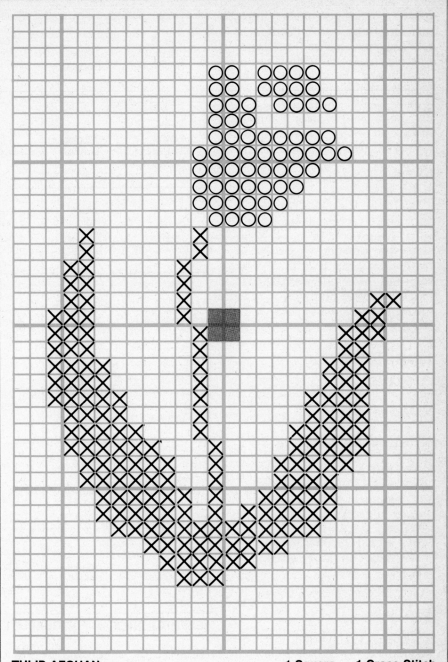

TULIP AFGHAN   **1 Square = 1 Cross-Stitch**
COLOR KEY
◎ **Peach Blossom (2870), Canary (2803), or Rose Heather (2837)**
⊠ **Peacock (2881)**

Cross-stitch 18 blocks using peacock for the leaves and stems and
stitch 6 tulips *each* with peach
blossom, canary, and rose heather. On graph paper, chart the mirror image of the same chart on a
40x40 block grid, noting the new
position of the block's center.
Work the remaining 18 blocks in
the same colors from your chart.

    ASSEMBLY: With Size H cro-
chet hook and peach blossom
yarn, work 1 rnd of sc around
each block working 2 sc in each
corner and approximately 37 sc
along each side; join with sl st to
first sc; fasten off.

    With wrong sides facing, sc 2
blocks tog, inserting hook in the
front lps only to create a ridge on
the front side of the work. Crochet
continued

6 blocks of same colored tulips, all facing in the same direction, to make 1 row; assemble 6 rows. Crochet rows tog. The finished afghan is 6 blocks wide by 6 blocks long in the following color sequence: Row 1 contains 6 blocks of canary tulips; Row 2 has 6 blocks of peach blossom tulips; Row 3 has 6 blocks of rose heather tulips; rows 4–6 repeat rows 1–3 in the same color sequence.

BORDER: With peach blossom and Size H crochet hook, join yarn in any corner st, ch 3, in same st work 4 dc; * sk 2 sts, sc in next st, sk 2 sts, 5 dc in next st; rep from * around, working 5 dc in each corner; join with sl st to top of beg ch-3; fasten off.

Bobble Block Afghan

Shown on page 61.

Afghan measures 46x64 inches.

MATERIALS
Unger Aries (3.5-ounce skein):
   11 skeins of white; 2 skeins *each* of peach, blue, and yellow
Size J afghan crochet hook or size to obtain gauge given below
Size H crochet hook

Abbreviations: See page 7.
Gauge: Each block measures 8½ inches square.

INSTRUCTION
BOBBLE SQUARE: With white yarn and Size J afghan hook, ch 28.
Row 1 (first half): Keeping all lps on hook, insert hook in top lp of second ch from hook, yo, draw up lp; * insert hook in top lp of next ch, yo, draw up lp; rep from * across row—28 lps on hook.
Row 1 (second half): Yo, draw through first lp on hook; * yo, draw through 2 lps on hook; rep from * across row until 1 lp rem on hook.

Blue Bobble	White Bobble	Yellow Flower With Peach Leaves	Yellow Bobble	Yellow Flower With Blue Leaves
Yellow Flower With Peach Leaves	3-Color Bobble	White Bobble	Blue Flower With Peach Leaves	White Bobble
White Bobble	Blue Flower With Peach Leaves	Peach Bobble	White Bobble	Blue Flower With Yellow Leaves
Yellow and Blue Bobble	White Bobble	Yellow Flower With Blue Leaves	3-Color Bobble	White Bobble
Peach Flower With Blue Leaves	Peach Bobble	White Bobble	Peach Flower With Blue Leaves	Blue Bobble
Peach and Blue Bobble	Blue Flower With Yellow Leaves	3-Color Bobble	White Bobble	Peach Flower With Yellow Leaves
White Bobble	Yellow Bobble	Peach Flower With Yellow Leaves	Peach And Yellow Bobble	White Bobble

ASSEMBLY DIAGRAM FOR BOBBLE BLOCK AFGHAN

Row 2 (first half): Keeping all lps on hook, sk first bar, * insert hook in next bar and draw up lp; rep from * across—28 lps on hook.
Row 2: (second half): Yo, draw through the first lp on the hook; yo, draw through 2 lps on hook; * ch 3, (yo, draw through 2 lps on hook) 2 times; rep from * across row until 1 lp rem on hook.
Row 3 (first half): Rep first half of Row 2, taking care that the ch-3 lps (bobbles) pop out on front side of work.
Row 3 (second half): Yo, draw through the first lp on the hook; * (yo, draw through 2 lps on hook) 2 times; ch 3; rep from * across until 1 lp rem on hook.
Rep rows 2 and 3 for pat until piece measures 8¼ inches.
Last row: Sk first bar, * **draw up lp in next bar and draw yarn through lp on hook—sl st made and 1 lp on hook;** rep from * across; fasten off.

Work 10 more bobble blocks with white yarn, taking care to have the same number of rows on each block.

Make bobble blocks in assorted colors as follows: 2 *each* in solid peach, blue, and yellow; 3 blocks using the 3 yarn colors in alternate rows; 1 block using peach

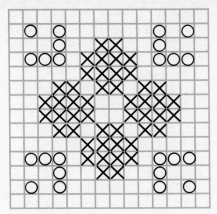

DUPLICATE STITCH CHART

☐ Leaf
☒ Flower

and yellow in alternate rows; 1 block using peach and blue; and 1 block using yellow and blue.

STOCKINETTE STITCH BLOCK (make 12): With white yarn and Size J afghan hook, ch 28.

Row 1 (first and second halves): Rep Row 1 of Bobble Block.

Row 2 (first half): Ch 1, * **insert hook from front, through center of next vertical lp, to the back of the work, yo, draw up lp—k st made;** rep from * across row.

Row 2 (second half): Yo, draw through first lp on hook; * yo, draw through 2 lps on hook; rep from * across until 1 lp rem on hook.

Rep Row 2 for pat until block measures 8½ inches square (approximately 30 rows).

EMBROIDERY: Referring to chart, *above,* work duplicate stitches in color combinations as shown on the block assembly diagram on page 70. Refer to page 31 for diagram to work the duplicate stitching.

BLOCK ASSEMBLY: With Size H hook, join white yarn and sc evenly spaced around all blocks; work approximately 26 sc on each side and 3 sc in each corner; join with sl st to first sc; fasten off.

Lay blocks as shown in the diagram on page 70. Insert Size H hook into corner sts of 2 blocks to be joined together, yo, draw lp

through sts, pull tightly; * ch 3, sk next sc on top block, sl st in next sc on top; sk next sc on bottom block, sl st in next sc on bottom; rep from * to corner; sl st the 2 corner sts tog; fasten off.

Continue to join blocks in this fashion. Assemble 5 strips of 7 blocks in each. Then join strips together in the same manner, taking care to line up all horizontal lines.

BORDER: *Rnd 1:* With white, work 1 rnd of sc around entire afghan, working approximately 144 sc along the short sides and 207 sc along the long sides and 4 sc in each corner; join with sl st to first sc.

Rnds 2 and 3: Working in back lps of each st, sc in each sc around; join to first sc.

Rnd 4: Ch 1, sc in same st as join; * ch 3, sk next sc, sl st in next sc; rep from * around; join to first sc; fasten off.

Trip-Around-the-World Lap Robe

Shown on page 63.

Lap robe measures 39x41 inches.

MATERIALS
Coats & Clark Red Heart 4-ply knit and crochet yarn (3.5-ounce skein) in the following amounts and colors: 2 skeins *each* of yellow (No. 230), skipper blue (No. 848), robin blue (No. 814), and off-white (No. 3); 3 skeins of maize (No. 261)
Size G afghan crochet hook
Size G crochet hook
Yarn tapestry needle

Abbreviations: See page 7.
Gauge: 8 sts and 7 rows in afghan stitch = 2 inches.

INSTRUCTIONS
Note: Lap robe is composed of 15 strips that are joined together as they are worked. Each strip has 15 colored blocks. Each colored block has 8 rows of afghan

stitch that are worked over 10 stitches. Refer to diagram on page 72 for easy reference to colors and placement of blocks as you work.

FIRST STRIP: With robin blue, ch 10.

Row 1 (first half): Keeping all lps on hook, insert hook in top lp of second ch from hook, yo, draw up lp; * insert hook in top lp of next ch, yo, draw up lp; rep from * across row—10 lps on hook.

Row 1 (second half): Yo, draw through first lp on hook, * yo, draw through 2 lps on hook; rep from * across row until 1 lp rem on hook.

Row 2 (first half): Keeping all lps on hook, sk first upright bar, * insert hook in next bar and draw up lp; rep from * across row—10 lps on hook.

Row 2 (second half): Rep second half of Row 1.

Rows 3–8: Rep Row 2. At end of Row 8, work until 2 lps rem on hook; drop robin blue yarn to back of work; **make a slip knot with maize and draw maize lp through last 2 lps on hook— yarn color change made.**

Work 8 rows with maize yarn, changing to yellow at end of eighth row.

Continue to work in this manner, working in the following color sequence to complete the first strip: skipper blue, off-white, maize, robin blue, yellow, robin blue, maize, off-white, skipper blue, yellow, maize, and robin blue.

Work the eighth row of the last block (robin blue) as follows: Sk first bar, * **insert hook in next bar, yo, draw lp through bar and lp on hook—sl st made and 1 lp on hook;** rep from * across row; fasten off.

SECOND STRIP: With maize, ch 10.

Row 1 (first half): Keeping all lps on hook, insert hook in top lp of second ch from hook, yo, draw up lp; * insert hook in top lp of next ch, yo, draw up lp; rep from * across row—10 lps on hook. Join

continued

work to first strip as follows: Insert hook from front to back through the first st at end of corresponding row on *first* strip, yo, draw up lp—11 lps on hook.

Row 1 (second half): * Yo, draw through 2 lps on hook; rep from * across until 1 lp rem on hook.

Continue to work and join 8 rows of each color of this strip to the corresponding row on the first strip in the following color sequence: maize, yellow, skipper blue, off-white, maize, robin blue, yellow, skipper blue, yellow, robin blue, maize, off-white, skipper blue, yellow, and maize; sl st across the last row and join to previous strip with a sl st.

Work all rem strips as for Second Strip as follows:

THIRD STRIP: Yellow, skipper blue, off-white, maize, robin blue, yellow, skipper blue, off-white, skipper blue, yellow, robin blue, maize, off-white, skipper blue, and yellow.

FOURTH STRIP: Skipper blue, off-white, maize, robin blue, yellow, skipper blue, off-white, maize, off-white, skipper blue, yellow, robin blue, maize, off-white, and skipper blue.

FIFTH STRIP: Off-white, maize, robin blue, yellow, skipper blue, off-white, maize, yellow, maize, off-white, skipper blue, yellow, robin blue, maize, and off-white.

SIXTH STRIP: Maize, robin blue, yellow, skipper blue, off-white, maize, yellow, robin blue, yellow, maize, off-white, skipper blue, yellow, robin blue, and maize.

SEVENTH STRIP: Robin blue, yellow, skipper blue, off-white, maize, yellow, robin blue, skipper blue, robin blue, yellow, maize, off-white, skipper blue, yellow, and robin blue,.

EIGHTH STRIP: Yellow, skipper blue, off-white, maize, yellow, robin blue, skipper blue, robin blue, skipper blue, robin blue, yellow, maize, off-white, skipper blue, and yellow.

NINTH STRIP: Rep Seventh Strip.

TENTH STRIP: Rep Sixth Strip.

ELEVENTH STRIP: Rep Fifth Strip.

TWELFTH STRIP: Rep Fourth Strip.

THIRTEENTH STRIP: Rep Third Strip.

FOURTEENTH STRIP: Rep Second Strip.

FIFTEENTH STRIP: Rep First Strip.

Tie loose ends tog. With yarn needle, weave ends under joining stitches, matching thread colors.

BORDER: *Rnd 1:* With right side facing and Size G hook, join maize in corner st of last robin blue block, ch 1, 3 sc in same st; working across the bound-off edge, * sc in next 8 sts, draw up lp in each of next 2 sts (joining stitches), yo, and draw through 3 lps on hook; rep from * to next corner. Work 3 sc in corner st. Sc in each st across the next side. Work the rem 2 sides to correspond; join to first sc; do not turn.

Rnd 2: Ch 1, sc in same st as join, mark this sc. * Working in back lps, sc in each st to corner, 3 sc in corner; rep from * around; do not join.

Rnds 3–7: Rep Rnd 2, marking first st of each rnd and working in back lps. At end of Row 7, join with sl st to first sc; fasten off.

Rnd 8: With right side facing, join robin blue in any corner st, ch 1, 3 sc in same st; * sc in each st to corner st, 3 sc in corner st; rep from * around; join with sl st to first sc.

Rnd 9: Working from left to right (reverse sc) and crocheting under both lps, * ch 1, sk sc, sc in next sc; rep from * to 3 corner sc; (sc in next sc, ch 1) 3 times. Rep from first * around; join to first sc; fasten off.

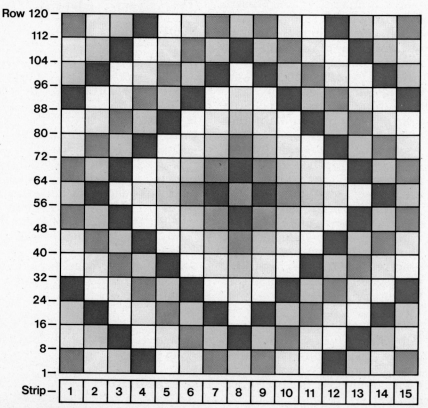

TRIP-AROUND-THE-WORLD LAP ROBE

COLOR KEY

☐ Yellow (230)   ☐ Off-White (3)   ☐ Maize (261)
■ Skipper Blue (848)   ▨ Robin Blue (814)

Aunt Sukie's Choice Lap Robe

Shown on page 62.

Robe measures 32½x49 inches.

MATERIALS

Coats & Clark Red Heart Caress 4-ply brushed yarn (3-ounce skein) in the following amounts and colors: 4 skeins of ivory (I) (No. 102); 3 skeins of royal blue (RB) (No. 848); 1 skein *each* of boysenberry (B) (No. 594); soft blue (SB) (No. 818); lilac (L) (No. 576); and light violet (LV) (No. 584)
Size G afghan crochet hook
Size G crochet hook
Yarn tapestry needle

Abbreviations: See page 7.
Gauge: 7 rows and 8 sts in afghan stitch = 2 inches.

INSTRUCTIONS

Note: Lap robe is composed of 12 strips that are joined together as they are worked. Each strip has 18 colored blocks. Each colored block has 8 rows of basic afghan crochet stitches. Refer to diagram on page 75 for easy reference to color placement of blocks as you work.

FIRST STRIP: With L, ch 8.
Row 1 (first half): Keeping all lps on hook, insert hook in top lp of second ch from hook, yo, draw up lp; * insert hook in top lp of next ch, yo, draw up lp; rep from * across row—8 lps on hook.
Row 1 (second half): Yo, draw through first lp on hook, * yo, draw through 2 lps on hook; rep from * across row until 1 lp rem on hook.
Row 2 (first half): Keeping all lps on hook, sk first upright bar, * insert hook in next bar and draw up lp; rep from * across row—8 lps on hook.
Row 2 (second half): Rep second half of Row 1.
Rows 3–8: Rep Row 2. At end of Row 8, work until 2 lps rem on hook; drop L yarn to back of work; **make a slip knot with I and draw I lp through last 2 lps**

on hook—yarn color change made. Cut L, leaving a 4-inch strand.
Rows 9–16: Rep Row 2 with I, changing to RB at end of Row 16. Do not cut I.
Note: The lp rem at the end of the second half of all rows *always* counts as the first st of the next row.
Row 17: Drop RB to back of work; sk first bar, draw up 7 lps with I; work second half of row with I until 2 lps rem on hook; with RB, draw through last 2 lps.
Row 18: Sk first bar, draw up lp in next bar with RB—2 RB lps on hook; drop RB to back of work; draw up lps in next 6 bars with I. On second half of row, work off 6 lps with I, drop I to back of work, draw off rem 2 lps with RB.
Row 19: Work first 3 sts with RB, last 5 sts with I.
Row 20: Work first 4 sts with RB, last 4 sts with I.
Row 21: Work first 5 sts with RB, last 3 sts with I.
Row 22: Work first 6 sts with RB, last 2 sts with I.
Row 23: Work first 7 sts with RB, last st with I.
Rows 24 and 25: Work all 8 sts with RB.
Rows 26–31: Work in reverse sequence, working 1 less stitch with RB in each row and 1 more stitch with I—at end of Row 31 there are 2 sts with RB and 6 stitches with I.
Row 32: Work 1 st with RB, 7 sts with I; on second half of row, use I to draw through all lps. Cut RB.
Rows 33–64: Work in pat with I. At end of Row 64, draw through last 2 lps with RB; do not cut I.
Rows 65–112: Rep rows 17–64.
Rows 113–128: Rep rows 17–32 in same color sequence.
Rows 129–136: Work in pat with I. At end of Row 136, draw through last 2 lps with LV; cut I.
Rows 137–144: Work in pat with LV for 7 rows. On the next row (bind off row), work as follows: Sk first bar, * **insert hook in next bar, yo, draw lp through bar and lp on hook—sl st made and 1 lp on hook;** rep from * across; fasten off.

SECOND STRIP: With I, ch 8.
Row 1 (first half): Keeping all lps on hook, insert hook in top lp of second ch from hook, yo, draw up lp; * insert hook in top lp of next ch, yo, draw up lp; rep from * across row—8 lps on hook. Join work to first strip as follows: Insert hook from front to back through the first st at the end of the corresponding row on the first strip, yo, draw up lp—9 lps on hook.
Row 1 (second half): * Yo, draw through 2 lps on hook; rep from * across until 1 lp rem on hook.
Continue to join each row of this strip and the succeeding strips to the corresponding row of the previous strip.
Rows 2–16: Work in pat with I. At end of Row 16, work until 2 lps rem on hook; drop I to back of work and draw B through last 2 lps; cut I.
Row 17: Drop B to back of work; with SB, draw up lps in the next 7 bars; join to first strip. On second half of row, work off 7 sts with SB, 1 st with B.
Row 18: Work 2 sts with B, 6 sts with SB; join to first strip.
Row 19: Work 3 sts with B, 5 sts with SB; join to first strip.
Row 20: Work 4 sts with B, 4 sts with SB; join to first strip.
Row 21: Work 5 sts with B, 3 sts with SB; join to first strip.
Row 22: Work 6 sts with B, 2 sts with SB; join to first strip.
Row 23: Work 7 sts with B, 1 st with SB; join to first strip.
Rows 24 and 25: Work all 8 sts with B; join to first strip.
Row 26: Work 7 sts with B, 1 st with SB; join to first strip.
Rows 27–31: Work in reverse sequence, working 1 less stitch with B in each row and 1 more stitch with SB—at end of Row 31 there are 2 sts with B and 6 stitches with SB.
Row 32: Work 1 st with B, 7 sts with SB; on second half of row, use I to draw through last 2 lps on hook. Cut B and SB yarns.
Rows 33–48: Work 8 sts with I.
Rows 49–144: Rep rows 1–48 twice, working Row 1 in the basic st. Bind off last row; join to previous strip with sl st; fasten off.

continued

THIRD STRIP: With I, ch 8.

Row 1: Work 8 sts with I, changing to RB at end of row.

Rows 2-7: Cont in pat, working 1 more st each row with RB and 1 less stitch with I—at end of Row 7 there are 7 sts with RB and 1 st with I.

Row 8: Work 8 sts with RB, changing to B at end of row; cut RB and I.

Row 9: Drop B to back of work, with SB, draw up a lp in next 7 sts. On second half of row, work 7 sts with SB, 1 st with B.

Rows 10-15: Cont in pat, working 1 more st in each row with B and 1 less stitch with SB—at end of Row 15 there are 7 sts with B and 1 st with SB.

Row 16: Work 8 sts with B, changing to LV at end of row; cut B and SB.

Rows 17-24: Work all sts with LV; change to L at end of Row 24; cut LV.

Rows 25-32: Work all sts with L; change to B at end of Row 32; cut L.

Row 33: Work all 8 sts with B.

Row 34: Work 7 sts with B, 1 st with SB.

Rows 35-40: Cont in pat, working 1 more st in each row with SB and 1 less st with B; change to RB at end of Row 40; cut B and SB.

Row 41: Work all sts with RB.

Row 42: Work 7 sts with RB, 1 st with I.

Rows 43-48: Cont in pat, working 1 more st in each row with I and 1 less st with RB—at end of Row 48 there is 1 st with RB and 7 sts with I.

Rows 49-64: Rep rows 1-16, changing to L at end of Row 64.

Rows 65-72: Work all sts with L, changing to LV at end of last row; cut L.

Rows 73-80: Work with LV, changing to B at end of last row; cut LV.

Rows 81-96: Rep rows 33-48.

Rows 97-144: Rep rows 1-47; bind off with I.

FOURTH STRIP: With I, ch 8.

Row 1: Draw up 6 lps with I—7 lps on hook; drop I to back of work, draw up 1 lp with RB; join to previous strip. Work off 1 st with RB, 7 sts with I.

Rows 2-7: Cont in pat, working 1 more st in each row with RB and 1 less st with I.

Row 8: Work 8 sts with RB; change to SB at end of row; cut RB and I.

Row 9: Draw up 6 lps with SB—7 lps on hook; 1 st with B.

Rows 10-15: Cont in pat, working 1 more st in each row with SB and 1 less st with B.

Rows 16: 8 sts with B; change to L at end of row; cut SB and B.

Rows 17-24: Work in pat with L; change to LV on last row; cut L.

Rows 25-32: Work all sts with LV; change to B on last row; cut LV.

Row 33: Work 8 sts with B, changing to SB at end of row.

Row 34: Work 1 st with SB, 7 sts with B.

Rows 35-40: Cont in pat, working 1 more st in each row with SB and 1 less st with B; change to RB at end of Row 41; cut SB and B.

Row 41: Work 8 sts with RB, changing to I at end of row.

Row 42: Work 1 st with I, 7 sts with RB.

Rows 43-48: Cont in pat, working 1 more st in each row with I and 1 less st with RB.

Rows 49-64: Rep rows 1-16, changing to LV at end of Row 64.

Rows 65-72: Work in pat with LV, changing to L at end of Row 72; cut LV.

Rows 73-80: Work in pat with L, changing to B at end of Row 80; cut L.

Rows 81-96: Rep rows 33-48.

Rows 97-144: Rep rows 1-48; bind off with I on last row.

FIFTH STRIP: With I, ch 8.

Rows 1-16: Rep rows 1-16 of Strip 2, changing to SB at end of Row 16; cut I.

Rows 17-23: Rep rows 9-15 of Fourth Strip.

Row 24: Work 8 sts with B.

Rows 25-32: Rep rows 33-40 of Strip 4, changing to I at end of Row 32; cut SB and B.

Rows 33-48: Cont in pat and work all sts with I.

Rows 49-144: Rep rows 1-48 twice; bind off on last row.

SIXTH STRIP: With I, ch 8.

Rows 1-16: Work in pat with I.

Row 17: Work 7 sts with I, 1 st with RB.

Rows 18-23: Cont in pat, working 1 more st in each row with RB and 1 less st with I.

Row 24: Work 8 sts with RB.

Row 25: Work 8 sts with RB, changing to I at end of row.

Rows 26-32: Cont in pat, working 1 more st in each row with I and 1 less st with RB; cut RB.

Rows 33-40: Work all sts with I; change to LV at end of Row 40; cut I.

Rows 41-48: Work all sts with LV; change to L at end of Row 48; cut LV.

Rows 49-56: Work all sts with L; change to I at end of Row 56; cut L.

Rows 57-88: Rep rows 1-40; change to L at end of Row 88; cut I.

Rows 89-96: Work all sts with L; change to LV at end of Row 96; cut L.

Rows 97-104: Work all sts with LV; change to I at end of Row 104; cut LV.

Rows 105-112: Work all sts with I.

Rows 113-128: Rep rows 17-32.

Rows 129-144: Work all sts with I; bind off last row.

SEVENTH STRIP: With I, ch 8.

Rows 1-16: Work in pat with I, changing to RB at end of Row 16.

Rows 17-32: Rep rows 17-32 of First Strip.

Rows 33-40: Work in pat with I, changing to L at end of Row 40; cut I.

Rows 41-48: Work in pat with L, changing to LV at end of Row 48; cut L.

Rows 49-56: Work in pat with LV, changing to I at end of Row 56; cut LV.

Rows 57-64: Work in pat with I, changing to RB at end of Row 64.

Rows 65-88: Rep rows 17-40 of this strip, changing to LV at end of Row 88; cut I.

Rows 89-96: Work in pat with LV, changing to L at end of Row 96; cut LV.

Rows 97–104: Work in pat with L, changing to I at end of Row 104; cut L.

Rows 105–112: Work in pat with I, changing to RB at end of Row 112.

Rows 113–128: Rep rows 17–32 of this strip.

Rows 129–144: Work in pat with I; bind off last row.

EIGHTH STRIP: Rep Second Strip.

NINTH STRIP: With I, ch 8.

Rows 1–16: Rep rows 1–16 of Third Strip, changing to L at end of Row 16.

Rows 17–24: Work in pat with L, changing to LV at end of Row 24; cut L.

Rows 25–32: Work in pat with LV, changing to B at end of Row 32; cut LV.

Rows 33–64: Rep rows 33–64 of Third Strip, changing to LV at end of Row 64.

Rows 65–72: Work in pat with LV, changing to L at end of Row 72; cut LV.

Rows 73–80: Work in pat with L, changing to B at end of Row 80; cut L.

Rows 81–112: Rep rows 33–64 of Third Strip, changing to L at end of Row 112.

Rows 113–144: Rep rows 17–48 of Third Strip; bind off.

TENTH STRIP: With I, ch 8.

Rows 1–16: Rep rows 1–16 of Fourth Strip; changing to LV at end of Row 16.

Rows 17–24: Work in pat with LV, changing to L at end of Row 24; cut LV.

Rows 25–32: Work in pat with L, changing to B at end of Row 32; cut L.

Row 33–48: Rep rows 33–48 of Fourth Strip.

Rows 49–64: Rep rows 1–16, changing to L at end of Row 64.

Rows 65–72: Work in pat with L, changing to LV at end of Row 72; cut L.

Rows 73–80: Work in pat with LV, changing to B at end of Row 80; cut LV.

Rows 81–96: Rep rows 33–48.

Rows 97–144: Rep rows 1–48; bind off with I on last row.

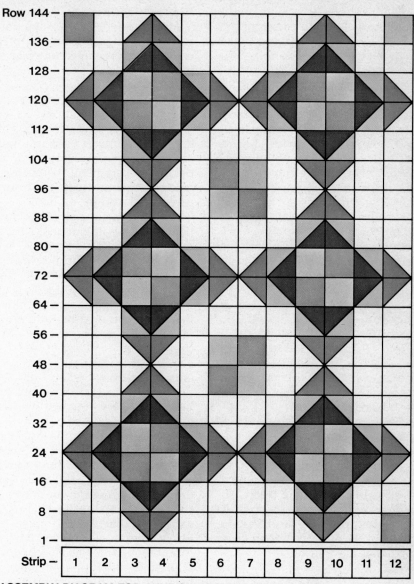

ASSEMBLY DIAGRAM FOR AUNT SUKIE'S CHOICE LAP ROBE

■ Royal Blue—RB (848) ■ Boysenberry—BB (594) ▨ Lilac—L (576)
□ Soft Blue—SB (818) ▨ Light Violet—LV (584) □ Ivory—I(102)

ELEVENTH STRIP: Rep Fifth Strip.

TWELTH STRIP: With LV, ch 8.

Rows 1–8: Work in pat with LV, changing to I at end of Row 8.

Rows 9–16: Work even in pat with I.

Rows 17–32: Rep Rows 17–32 of Sixth Strip.

Rows 33–64: Cont to work in pat with I.

Rows 65–112: Rep rows 17–64.

Rows 113–128: Rep rows 17–32 of Sixth Strip.

Rows 129–136: Work in pat with I, changing to L at end of Row 136.

Rows 137–144: Work in pat with L; bind off last row.

FINISHING: Tie loose yarn ends together and use yarn needle to weave yarns under matching colors of joining stitches.

continued

BORDER: *Rnd 1:* With right side facing, join I in corner of the last L row, ch 1, 3 sc in same st; * sc in next 6 sts, at the joining (insert hook in next st, pull up lp) twice, yo, draw through 3 lps on hook; rep from * to next corner, 3 sc in corner; sc in each st along next side; 3 sc in corner; rep from first * around; end with sl st in back lp of first sc; do not turn.

Rnd 2: Ch 1, working in back lps, sc in same st as joining (mark st); * 3 sc in corner st, sc in each st to next corner; rep from * around; do not join.

Rnds 3–8: Cont to sc in back lps only and mark the first st of each rnd; work 3 sc in each corner st; at end of Rnd 8, sc to the center st of next corner; join with sl st in back lp of center st; fasten off I; do not turn.

Rnds 9–12: Join RB in same st as join, ch 1, 3 sc in same st (mark first st); rep Rnd 2. At end of Rnd 12, join to first st with sl st under both lps; do not turn.

Rnd 13: Working under both lps, ch 3; in same st work dc, ch 1, and 2 dc; sk st, sc in next st, sk st, in center st at corner work 3 dc, ch 1, and 3 dc; * sk st, sc in next st, sk st, in next st work 2 dc, ch 1, and 2 dc; rep from * around, working 3 dc, ch 1, and 3 dc in each corner st; join with sl st to top of beg ch-3; fasten off.

Aran Afghan

Shown on pages 64 and 65.

Afghan measures 52x62 inches, excluding fringe.

MATERIALS

Brunswick Germantown (3.5-ounce skein): 16 skeins of Sea Oats Heather (No. 4281)
Size 10 (J) afghan crochet hook
Size I crochet hook

Abbreviations: See page 7.
Gauge: 7 afghan sts = 2 inches.

INSTRUCTIONS

Afghan is worked in 3 separate panels. When panels are completed, they are crocheted together to make 1 piece.

AFGHAN PANEL (make 3): With afghan crochet hook, ch 65.

Row 1 (first half): Keeping all lps on hook, insert hook in top lp of second ch from hook, yo, draw up lp; * insert hook in top lp of next ch, yo, draw up lp; rep from * across row—65 lps on hook.

Row 1 (second half): Yo, draw through first lp on hook, * yo, draw through 2 lps on hook; rep from * across row until 1 lp rem on hook.

Row 2 (first half): Keeping all lps on hook, sk first upright bar, * insert hook in next bar and draw up lp; rep from * across row—65 lps on hook.

Row 2 (second half): Rep second half of Row 1.

Note: All subsequent second halves of every row are worked following second half of Row 1.

Row 3 (first half): Sk first bar, draw up lp in next bar; **yo hook twice, draw up lp around bar 2 rows below the next bar, (yo, draw through 2 lps on hook) 2 times—foundation post st (fps) made;** sk bar behind post st, (draw up lp in each of next 9 bars, fps around bar 2 rows below next st) 2 times; draw up lp in each of next 19 bars, (fps around bar 2 rows below next st, draw up lp in each of next 9 bars) 2 times; fps around bar 2 rows below next st, draw up lp in last 2 bars. Work second half of row.

Row 4: Rep Row 2.

Row 5 (first half): Sk first bar, draw up lp in next bar, **yo hook twice, draw up lp around post st below, (yo, draw through 2 lps on hook) 2 times—front post (fp) made;** sk st behind fp, draw up lp in next 4 bars; **yo, draw up lp in next bar, yo, draw up lp in same bar, yo, draw through 4 lps on hook, ch 1—popcorn (pc) made;** draw up lp in next 4 bars; (fp around post st, draw up lp in next 9 bars) 2 times; pc in next bar; (draw up lp in next 9 bars, fp around post st) 2 times; draw up lp in next 4 bars, pc in next bar; draw up lp in next 4 bars, fp around post st, draw up lp in next 2 bars. Work second half of row.

Row 6 (first half): Sk first bar, draw up lps in next 5 bars; (pc in next bar, draw up lp in next bar) 2 times; * draw up lps in next 21 bars, (pc in next bar, draw up lp in next bar) 2 times; rep from * once more; draw up lps in last 5 bars. Work second half of row.

Row 7 (first half): Sk first bar, draw up lp in next bar; fp around post st below, draw up lp in next 4 bars, pc in next bar; draw up lp in next 4 bars; fp around next post st, draw up lp in next 9 bars; fp around next post st, draw up lp in 7 bars; pc in next bar, draw up lp in 3 bars; pc in next bar, draw up 7 lps, fp around post st below, draw up 9 lps, fp around next post st, draw up 4 lps, pc in next bar, draw up 4 lps, fp around post st below, draw up 2 lps. Work second half of row.

Row 8 (first half): Sk first bar, draw up 28 lps, pc in next bar, draw up 5 lps, pc in next bar, draw up 29 lps. Work second half of row.

Row 9: Sk first bar, draw up lp in next bar, (fp around post st below, draw up 9 lps) 2 times; fp around post st below, draw up 5 lps, pc in next bar, draw up 7 lps, pc in next bar, draw up 5 lps, (fp around post st below, draw up 9 lps) 2 times; fp around post st below, draw up 2 lps. Work second half of row.

Row 10: Sk first bar, draw up 26 lps, pc in next bar, draw up 9 lps, pc in next bar, draw up 27 lps. Work second half of row.

Row 11 (first half): Sk first bar, draw up lp in next bar; fp around post st below, draw up 9 lps, fp around post st below, draw up 4 lps; **working 3 rows below and retaining last lp of each trc on hook, work 1 trc in each of the fourth, fifth, and sixth bars of this 9-st panel, yo, draw through 3 lps on hook—cluster made;** sk bar behind cluster, draw up 4 lps; fp around post st below, draw up 3 lps, pc in next bar, draw up 11 lps, pc in next bar, draw up 3 lps, fp around post st below, draw up 4 lps, work cluster, draw up 4 lps, fp around post st below, draw up 9 lps, fp around post st below, draw up 2 lps. Work second half of row.

Row 12 (first half): Rep Row 10.

Row 13 (first half): Sk first bar, draw up lp in next bar, fp around post st below, draw up 4 lps, pc in next bar, draw up 4 lps, fp around post st below, draw up 9 lps, fp around post st below, draw up 5 lps, pc in next bar, draw up 3 lps, **retaining last lp of each trc on hook, work trc around eighth bar of the diamond panel of Row 11, trc around ninth bar of Row 10, ch 1, work double trc (yo hook 3 times) around 10th bar of Row 9, trc around 11th bar of Row 10, ch 1, trc around 12th bar of Row 11, yo, draw through 5 lps on hook—large cluster made;** draw up 3 lps, pc in next bar, draw up 5 lps, fp around post st below, draw up 9 lps, fp around post st below, draw up 4 lps, pc in next bar, draw up 4 lps, fp around post st below, draw up 2 lps. Rep second half of row.

Row 14 (first half): Sk first bar, draw up 5 lps, (pc in next bar, draw up 1 lp) 2 times, draw up 19 lps, pc in next bar, draw up 5 lps, pc in next bar, draw up 20 lps, (pc in next bar, draw up 1 lp) 2 times; draw up 5 lps. Rep second half of row.

Row 15 (first half): Sk first bar, draw up lp in next bar, fp around post st below, draw up 4 lps, pc in next bar, draw up 4 lps, fp around post st below, draw up 9 lps, fp around post st below, draw up 7 lps, pc around next bar, draw up 3 lps, pc around next bar, draw up 7 lps, fp around post st below, draw up 9 lps, fp around post st below, draw up 4 lps, pc around next bar, draw up 4 lps, fp around next post st, draw up 2 lps. Rep second half of row.

Row 16 (first half): Sk first bar, draw up 30 lps, pc around next bar, draw up 1 lp, pc around next bar, draw up 31 lps. Rep second half of row.

Row 17 (first half): Sk first bar, draw up lp in next bar, (fp around post st below, draw up 9 lps) 3 times; pc in next bar, (draw up 9 lps, fp around post st below) 3 times; draw up 2 lps. Rep second half of row.

Row 18: Rep Row 2.

Row 19 (first half): Sk first bar, draw up 1 lp, fp around post st below, draw up 9 lps, fp around post st below, draw up 4 lps, work cluster, draw up 4 lps, fp around post st below, draw up 19 lps, fp around post st below, draw up 4 lps, work cluster, draw up 4 lps, fp around post st below, draw up 9 lps, fp around post st below, draw up 2 lps. Rep second half of row.

Row 20: Rep Row 2.

Rep rows 5–20 for panel pat. Work until 9 center diamond pats are complete; end with Row 20.

Last row: Sk first bar, * **draw up lp in next bar and draw yarn through lp on hook—sl st made;** rep from * across; fasten off.

FINISHING: With Size I hook and right side of panel facing, work row of sc around each panel, working 3 sc in each corner; fasten off.

Join panels by placing wrong sides of 2 panels tog; attach yarn at lower-left corner. Sc in first sc of both panels (inserting hook through first sc of both the top and bottom panels at the same time); ch 1, working from *left to right,* work sc, ch 1, into matching scs until 2 panels are attached; fasten off. Join third panel in same manner.

Join yarn to lower-left corner of outside edge and work in same pat to upper-right corner. Rep pat along opposite edge.

FRINGE: Cut yarn into 24-inch lengths. In bundles of 4 strands, fold strands in half and loop through every fourth st on short end of afghan. Using 4 strands from each of 2 adjoining tassels, knot tassels again approximately 1½ inches below previous knot.

Blue Diagonal Afghan

Shown on page 66.

Afghan measures 55 inches wide and 67 inches long.

MATERIALS
Brunswick Windrush (3.5-ounce skein) 12 skeins of Faded Denim Heather (No. 9072)
Size 10 (J) flexible afghan crochet hook
Size I crochet hook

Abbreviations: See page 7.
Gauge: 4 afghan sts = 1 inch.

INSTRUCTIONS
Afghan is worked in pattern of 24-stitch repeat that moves diagonally across.

With afghan hook, ch 196.

Row 1 (first half): Keeping all lps on hook, insert hook in top lp of second ch from hook, yo, draw up lp; * insert hook in top lp of next ch, yo, draw up lp; rep from * across row—196 lps on hook.

Row 1 (second half): Yo, draw through first lp on hook, * yo, draw through 2 lps on hook; rep from * across row until 1 lp rem on hook.

Row 2 (first half): Keeping all lps on hook, sk first upright bar, * insert hook in next bar and draw up lp; rep from * across row—196 lps on hook.

Row 2 (second half): Yo, draw through first lp on hook, yo, draw through 2 lps on hook; * **(ch 2, yo, draw through 5 lps, ch 1, for "eye"—star st made)** 3 times; ch 1, (yo, draw through 2 lps on hook) 12 times; rep from * across row; end rep bet ( )s 14 times instead of 12.

Row 3 (first half): Keeping all lps on hook, sk first upright bar; draw up lp in each of next 13 bars; * (draw up lp under ch-sp, draw up lp in ch-1 "eye," draw up lp in each of next 2 ch) 3 times; draw up lp in each of next 12 bars; rep from * across; end draw-up lp in each of last 2 bars.

Row 3 (second half): Rep second half of Row 2.

continued

Row 4 (first half): Rep first half of Row 3.

Row 4 (second half): Yo, draw through first lp on hook, (yo, draw through 2 lps on hook) 5 times; * work 3 star sts, ch 1, (yo, draw through 2 lps on hook) 12 times; rep from *; end (yo, draw through 2 lps on hook) 10 times.

Row 5 (first half): Sk first up-right bar, draw up lp in each of next 9 bars; * (draw up lp under ch-sp, draw up lp in ch-1 "eye," draw up lp in each of next 2 ch) 3 times; draw up lp in each of next 12 bars; rep from * across; end draw up lp in each of last 6 bars.

Row 5 (second half): Rep second half of Row 4.

Row 6 (first half): Rep first half of Row 5.

Row 6 (second half): Yo, draw through first lp on hook, (yo, draw through 2 lps on hook) 9 times; * work 3 star sts, ch 1, (yo, draw through 2 lps on hook) 12 times; rep from *; end (yo, draw through 2 lps on hook) 6 times.

Row 7 (first half): Sk first up-right bar, draw up lp in each of next 5 bars; * (draw up lp under ch-sp, draw up lp in ch-1 "eye," draw up lp in each of next 2 ch) 3 times; draw up lp in each of next 12 bars; rep from * across; end draw up lp in each of last 10 bars.

Row 7 (second half): Rep second half of Row 6.

Row 8 (first half): Rep first half of Row 7.

Row 8 (second half): Yo, draw through first lp on hook, (yo, draw through 2 lps on hook) 13 times; * work 3 star sts, ch 1, (yo, draw through 2 lps on hook) 12 times; rep from *; end (yo, draw through 2 lps on hook) 2 times.

Row 9 (first half): Sk first up-right bar, draw up lp in next bar; * (draw up lp under ch-sp, draw up lp in ch-1 "eye," draw up lp in each of next 2 ch) 3 times; draw up lp in each of next 12 bars; rep from * across; end draw up lp in each of last 14 bars.

Row 9 (second half): Rep second half of Row 8.

Row 10 (first half): Rep first half of Row 9.

Row 10 (second half): Yo, draw through first lp on hook, yo, draw through 2 lps on hook; work 1 star st, ch 1, * (yo, draw through 2 lps on hook) 12 times; work 3 star sts, ch 1; rep from *; end work 2 star sts, ch 1, (yo, draw through 2 lps on hook) 2 times.

Row 11 (first half): Sk first up-right bar, draw up lp in next bar; (draw up lp under ch-sp, draw up lp in ch-1 "eye," draw up lp in each of next 2 ch) 2 times; * draw up lp in each of next 12 bars; (draw up lp under ch-sp, draw up lp in ch-1 "eye," draw up lp in each of next 2 ch) 3 times; rep from *; end draw up 4 lps in star st and in each of last 2 bars.

Row 11 (second half): Rep second half of Row 10.

Row 12 (first half): Rep first half of Row 11.

Row 12 (second half): Yo, draw through first lp on hook, yo, draw through 2 lps on hook; work 2 star sts, ch 1, * (yo, draw through 2 lps on hook) 12 times; work 3 star sts, ch 1; rep from * across; end work 1 star st, ch 1, (yo, draw through 2 lps on hook) 2 times.

Row 13 (first half): Sk first up-right bar, draw up lp in next bar; draw up lp under ch-sp, draw up lp in ch-1 "eye," draw up lp in each of next 2 ch; * draw up lp in each of next 12 bars; (draw up lp under ch-sp, draw up lp in ch-1 "eye," draw up lp in each of next 2 ch) 3 times; rep from * across; end draw-up 8 lps in last 2 star sts and in each of last 2 bars.

Row 13 (second half): Rep second half of Row 12.

Rep rows 2–13 for pat 11 more times, then work rows 2–9.

Last row: Sk first bar, * **draw up lp in next bar and draw yarn through lp on hook—sl st made;** rep from * across; fasten off.

BORDER: With Size I hook, work sc evenly spaced around entire afghan, working 3 sc in each corner, taking care to keep work flat; join with sl st to first sc.

Rnd 1: Sc in back lp of each sc around, working 3 sc in center sc of each corner st; join to first sc.

Rnd 2: Ch 3, dc in back lp of each sc around, working 5 dc in center sc of each corner st; join with sl st to top of beg ch-3.

Rnds 3 and 4: Ch 1, sc in back lp of each st around, working 3 sc in center sc of each corner st; join to first sc.

Rnd 5: Ch 1, * sk 2 sc, 6 dc in next sc, sk 2 sc, sl st in next st; rep from * around taking care to work sl st in center sc of each corner; join with sl st in beg ch-1; fasten off. Weave in all loose ends.

Frosted Squares Afghan

Shown on page 67.
Afghan is 58 inches wide and 67 inches long.

MATERIALS
Caron Dazzleaire 4-ply yarn (3-ounce skein) in the following amounts and colors: 8 skeins of white (No. 2601), 2 skeins *each* of raspberry punch (No. 2686), azalea (No. 2628), crystal lilac (No. 2644), plum (No. 2831), baby green (No. 2834), and sky blue (No. 2620)
Size J afghan crochet hook
Size I crochet hook

Abbreviations: See page 7.
Gauge: 10 sts = 3 inches.

INSTRUCTIONS
For ease in working, crochet the colored squares first. Make 11 squares *each* from raspberry and green yarns; 8 squares *each* from azalea, plum, and blue yarns; and 10 squares from lilac yarn. Then add the white edging to each square, following the instructions for joining and referring to the chart on page 79 for color placement and block direction.

FIRST SQUARE: With afghan hook, ch 21.

Row 1 (first half): Keeping all lps on hook, insert hook in top lp of second ch from hook, yo, draw up lp; * insert hook in top lp of next ch, yo, draw up lp; rep from * across row—21 lps on hook.

Row 1 (second half): Yo, draw through first lp on hook; * yo, draw through 2 lps on hook; rep from * across row until 1 lp rem.

Row 2 (first half): Keeping all lps on hook, sk first bar, (**insert hook under next 2 bars, yo, draw yarn through both bars—dec made;** yo, draw up lp in each of next 2 bars) 5 times—21 lps on hook, counting each yo as lp.

Row 2 (second half): Rep second half of Row 1.

Row 3 (first half): Keeping all lps on hook, sk first bar, draw up lp in *each* of next 2 bars; (dec over next 2 bars, yo, draw up lp in *each* of next 2 bars) 4 times; end draw up lp in *each* of last 2 bars—21 lps on hook, counting yo as lp.

Row 3 (second half): Rep second half of Row 1.

Rows 4–13: Rep rows 2 and 3.

Row 14: Sc in each bar across, working under each bar and through back of each stitch; fasten off.

EDGING: *Rnd 1:* Join white yarn 1 stitch to the left of the upper-right corner of square. With I hook, * work 14 sc evenly spaced along side; work 3 sc in corner; rep from * 3 more times; join with sl st to first sc.

Rnd 2: Draw up lp on hook to ½ inch; yo, draw up ½-inch lp in same sc as sl st; yo, draw up ½-inch lp in next sc; yo, draw through 5 lps on hook; ch 1, * **(yo, draw up ½-inch lp in next sc) 2 times; yo, draw through all lps on hook ch 1—bobble made;** rep from * to corner—8 bobbles along side; ch 3, rep from first * 3 more times; end with ch 3, work 1 more bobble; join with sl st to ch-1 at beg of rnd; fasten off—9 bobbles on each side.

SECOND SQUARE: Work as for First Square until 3 sides of Rnd 2 of edging are worked, ending with ch-1 at corner.

Begin to join squares: With right sides facing up, sl st into ch-3 corner lp of First Square; ch 1, * work bobble, sl st into corresponding ch-1 of First Square; rep from * across side. At corner, ch 1, sl st into ch-3 of First Square, ch 1, work bobble along first side of square; fasten off.

Join next 5 squares to complete Row 1 of afghan.

EIGHTH SQUARE: Work same as Second Square and join to top of First Square. Join 15th, 22nd, 29th, 36th, 43rd, and 50th squares to top of first square in each succeeding row.

ALL REMAINING SQUARES: Work as established for Second Square, except work until 2 sides of Rnd 2 of edging are worked, ending with ch-1 at corner. Join to row as established; at corner, draw up lp in each of 3 corner sts, yo, and draw though all lps on hook. Work rem side as established and complete bobble on first side of square.

BORDER: *Rnd 1:* With wrong side facing and Size I hook, join white yarn in ch-1 st of any bobble, draw up lp on hook to ½ inch; * **yo, draw up lp in same ch-1 st, yo, draw up lp in ch-1 st of next bobble; yo, draw through all lps on hook—star stitch made;** ch 1 for "eye." Rep from * to corner. At corner, work star stitch over last bobble on square; in ch-3 corner lp work star stitch, ch 3, and star stitch; rep from first * around; ending with sl st in eye of first star stitch; ch 3, turn.

Rnd 2: * Dc in eye of next star stitch, ch 1; rep from * to corner; in corner ch-3 lp work dc, ch 3, and dc; ch 1; rep from first * around; join with sl st in third ch of beg ch-3. Do not turn.

Rnd 3: Draw up lp on hook to ½ inch, yo, draw up lp in same ch as sl st, yo, draw up lp in ch-1 sp; yo, draw through 5 lps on hook, ch 1; * yo, draw up lp in next dc, yo, draw up lp in next ch-1 sp, yo, draw though 5 lps on hook, ch 1; rep from * to corner. In corner ch-3 lp (yo, draw up lp) 2 times, yo, draw through all 5 lps on hook, ch 3; in same corner lp (yo, draw up lp) 2 times, yo, draw through 5 lps on hook; rep from first * around, working corners as established; join in beg ch-1; ch 1, turn.

Rnd 4: Draw up lp on hook to ½ inch and beg at *, rep Rnd 1; ch 3, turn.

Rnd 5: With right side facing and working from left to right, * sc in ch-1 st, ch 2; rep from * around; sc in each ch in ch-3 corners; join to beg sc; fasten off.

Row 8 E **Block 50**	D	C	B	A	F	E
7 A **Block 43**	F	E	D	C	B	A
6 C **Block 36**	B	A	F	E	D	C
5 E **Block 29**	D	C	B	A	F	E
4 A **Block 22**	F	E	D	C	B	A
3 C **Block 15**	B	A	F	E	D	C
2 E **Block 8**	D	C	B	A	F	E
1 A **Block 1**	F	E	D	C	B	A

FROSTED SQUARES AFGHAN

▨ Block Straight
☐ Block Turned

COLOR KEY

A—Raspberry C—Lilac E—Green
B—Azalea D—Plum F—Blue

ACKNOWLEDGMENTS

We would like to extend our special thanks to the following designers who contributed projects to this book.

Patricia Bevans—20–21, 22–23, 44–45, 46–47, 58–59

Judith Brandeau—40–41

Cathe Danna—62–63

Dixie Falls—4–5, 16–17, 18–19, 43, 61

Myrtle Larrison—24–25

Joyce Nordstrom—64–65, 66–67

Helene Rush—60

Karen Taylor—42

Mary Vermie for checking our patterns

We also are pleased to acknowledge the photographers whose talents and technical skills contributed much to this book.

Hopkins Associates—4–5, insets on pages 8–15, 16–17, 18–19, 22–23, 24–25, 40–41, 42–43, 44–45, 46–47, 62

Sean Fitzgerald—20–21, 58–59, 61, 62 (inset), 63, 64–65, 66–67

Michael Jensen—60

For their cooperation and courtesy, we extend a special thanks to the following industry sources for providing us with yarns and project assistance.

Aarlan Yarns
21 Adley Road
Cambridge, MA 02138
for afghan on pages 4–5

Bernat Yarn & Craft Corp.
Depot and Mendon Sts.
Uxbridge, MA 01569
for hats, scarves, and mittens on pages 22–23
for afghan on page 60

Brunswick Yarns
Brunswick Ave.
P.O. Box 548
Moosup, CT 06354
for afghans on pages 58–59, 64–65, 66

Caron International
Avenue E and First Street
Rochelle, IL 61068
for afghan on page 67

Coats & Clark Inc.
Dept. CS
P.O. Box 1010
Toccoa, GA 30577
for place mats and table runner on pages 20–21
for afghans on pages 62–63

DMC
P.O. Box 500
South Kearny, N.J. 07032-0500
for sachets on page 19

Susan Bates
212 Middlesex Ave.
Chester, CT 06412
for lingerie totes on pages 16–17
for pillow on page 18
for snowsuit on page 43
for coat on page 45
for sweater on page 46

Have BETTER HOMES AND GARDENS magazine delivered to your door. For information, write to:
MR. ROBERT AUSTIN
P.O. BOX 4536
DES MOINES, IA 50336